Canoeing Massachusetts, Rhode Island and Connecticut

On the Housatonic

Canoeing Massachusetts, Rhode Island and Connecticut

by Ken Weber

Photographs by
Lawrence S. Millard

Backcountry
Publications
Woodstock, Vermont

Acknowledgments

A special thanks to Manny Point and the other members of the Rhode Island Canoe Association for taking a flatlander from Ohio under their wings and showing him the wonders of whitewater canoeing. Also, a debt of gratitude is owed to Larry Millard, the photographer, who was my partner on these rivers. His companionship and wit were as valuable as his sparkling photographs in the completion of this book.

An invitation to the reader—

Rivers are notorious rearrangers of themselves and the objects they touch. Remember as you use this guide that water depths can vary considerably even from week to week, and that with time dams wash out, storms and floods rearrange rocks and channels, and new bridges and roads alter access points. If you run these rivers and find them changed from their descriptions here, please let the author and publisher know so that corrections may be made in future editions. Other comments and suggestions for additional river trips are also welcome. Address all correspondence:

Editor, Canoeing
Backcountry Publications
Box 175
Woodstock, VT 05091

Library of Congress Catalog Card Number: 79-90812
International Standard Book Number: 0-942440-14-5
© 1980 by Kenneth J. Weber
Tenth printing 1994, updated 1992
All rights reserved.
Published by Backcountry Publications
A division of The Countryman Press, Inc.
P.O. Box 175, Woodstock, VT 05091
Printed in the United States of America
Design by Wladislaw Finne
Back cover photograph by Michael Delaney

Map graphics by Kindler Design

Excerpt on page 9 reprinted, with permission, from
Beyond Your Doorstep: A Handbook to the Country,
by Hal Borland, © 1962, Alfred A. Knopf, Inc.

For my father, Frank Weber, who first introduced me to the fascination of flowing waters on our Sunday afternoon fishing outings so many years ago, and for my mother, Mary Weber, who taught me how to look at a river and see far more than water.

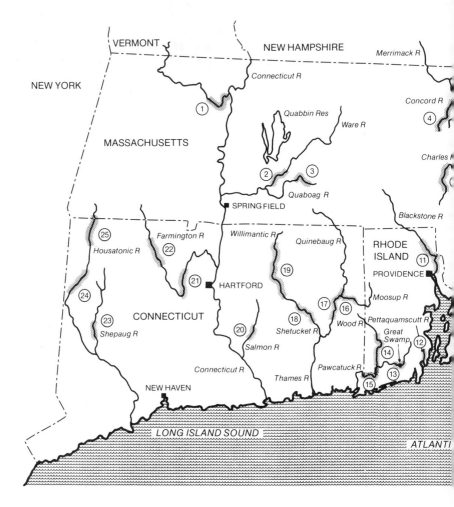

Contents

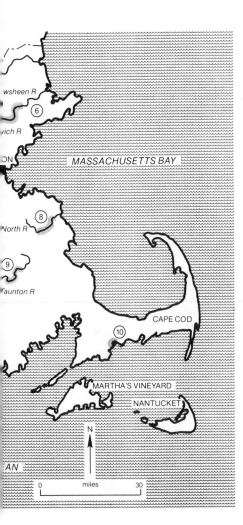

wsheen R

⑥

ich R

ON

MASSACHUSETTS BAY

⑧

North R

⑨

Taunton R

CAPE COD

⑩

MARTHA'S VINEYARD

NANTUCKET

N

AN

0   miles   30

Huge maples line the shore, providing the perfect canopy for a midsummer lunch break.

Introduction

"Any river is really the summation of a whole valley. It shapes not only the land but the life and even the culture of that valley. The trees that grow on its banks and all the greenness there may be common elsewhere but they still are special to that river. So are the birds, the insects, the animals that live along that river's banks. And the river has its own swarming life, its fish, its amphibians, its reptiles. To think of any river as nothing but water is to ignore the greater part of it."

—*Hal Borland,* Beyond Your Doorstep

This book is meant for those who share a fascination for moving waters. Whether you prefer tranquil streams or roaring whitewater rivers, you are kindred souls. The lure to follow that water, to float with it around the next bend, is irresistible.

Canoes provide that opportunity, particularly in New England, where few of the streams and rivers are large enough for other boats. However, the same problems seem to plague every canoeist—where to go and what to expect? You may be looking for a soothing day watching the birds along some quiet river, or you may want an exhilarating couple of hours shooting rapids. But most of all, you want to know what lies ahead. Having to carry around dams you didn't know existed can rob a trip of much of its enjoyment, and running into unexpected rapids can be very dangerous, especially for family groups or inexperienced canoeists. In addition, there is the headache of having to search for the best places to launch and take out your canoe. Many canoeists have wasted half their trip day on such details.

This book's purpose is to answer those questions. With twenty-five selected day trips there is something for everybody. In each case, details are provided not only for put-ins, take-outs, and the type of canoeing to expect, but also on the distance you'll be traveling, how long the trip should take you, the best time of year to make the trip, and what you are likely to see along the way. A sketch map and photographs also accompany each trip description to help you in your planning.

The charts that precede each trip show you at a glance what you generally can expect on that trip. In addition to the recommended put-ins and take-outs I have listed alternate access points so that you can plan shorter trips if necessary. Read the charts horizontally, following each line from the recommended put-in through the take-out point to the mileage and approximate paddling time. The last two categories at the far right show what kind of water conditions you can expect and the number of portages, if any, that you will encounter. The second line, then, shows similar information for what is usually a longer trip, most often starting from the same put-in but extending to a more distant take-out.

An example:

Put-in Point	Take-out Point	Approximate Distance	Approximate Trip Time	Condition of Water	Portages
Riverton picnic area	CT 318 bridge	4½ miles	2 hours	Minor rapids, smooth stretches	None
Riverton picnic area	Just above US 44 bridge	9½ miles	4-4½ hours	Minor rapids, smooth stretches, then mostly riffles	None

This chart, for the Upper Farmington River in Connecticut, shows that a trip from the picnic area in Riverton to the CT 318 bridge covers 4½ miles and should take you about 2 hours. The water features both minor rapids and smooth stretches. There are no portages. If a longer trip appeals to you, look at the second line. It shows that a journey from the same spot in Riverton to a take-out just above the US 44 bridge covers 9½ miles and should take about 4 to 4½ hours. The additional miles of water are mostly riffles. Again, there are no portages.

Which Rivers?

All parts of southern New England are represented. There are ten trips in Massachusetts, ten in Connecticut, and five in Rhode Island. On these trips you can travel on the cold, clean streams descending from the Berkshires or float on the sea-scented saltwater of Cape Cod; you can follow the routes of Thoreau in northeastern Massachusetts or enjoy the wild water in western Connecticut; and you can paddle beside sleek powerboats in eastern Rhode Island or move a few miles west and glide through a junglelike swamp.

How Far? How Long Will It Take?

The rivers were chosen for the variety they offer in geography, types of canoeing, and shoreline attractions. Each trip can be easily completed in a day. They range in length from about 3½ miles to 18 miles, with most covering approximately 8 to 10 miles. The estimates of the time each trip should take are based on my own experience on these rivers. Your time could be much faster or slower, depending on your interests, water conditions at the time you go, and what lures you to stop along the way. Generally, group trips take longer than trips involving just one or two canoes because of pauses to watch or assist newcomers and because groups usually take longer lunch breaks. Nearly all of the time estimates I have noted allow for lunch stops, which are integral parts of my own trips. The exceptions are the trips on the Moosup, the Pettaquamscutt, and the Blackstone, which can be completed easily in a couple of hours. In addition to trip time, be sure to allow time for car shuttling on one-way journeys. (Only one trip in this book, the Osterville-Grand Island trip on Cape Cod, ends where it begins.) Leaving a car at the take-out, driving on to the put-in, and later picking up both cars takes more time than most canoeists realize.

Safety Comes First: A Few Tips

Remember that this is a "where-to" guide, not a "how-to" book. It isn't necessary to be an expert canoeist to enjoy many of the trips recommended, but you should be familiar with basic canoeing skills and have a knowledge of safety rules. Canoeing courses are available in most communities, often through the American Red Cross, which also publishes canoeing booklets that emphasize safety. Common sense is as important as skill; don't attempt a whitewater river if you are a beginner in the sport.

If you are taking children along, it is wise to restrict your traveling to the calmer rivers. Insist that children remain seated at all times, limit your passengers (you should carry no more than two children or one adult in addition to you and your paddling partner), and be sure you know the swimming abilities of everyone in your canoe. Life preservers should be worn on all trips, and especially on whitewater rivers. Wetsuits—thick rubber suits worn next to the skin—should also be worn on whitewater trips because such trips of necessity must be made in early spring when the water is extremely cold. Wetsuits will help fend off the cold and reduce the threat of hypothermia—probably the greatest danger of early spring canoeing in southern New England. In addition, keep extra paddles and a first-aid kit secured inside your canoe.

Reading and Rating the River

Most of the rivers included in this book are usually smooth, but water conditions change dramatically with sudden spring thaws and heavy rains. Rivers run higher and faster at these times, and they can be dangerous. Keep this in mind when planning a trip, and look over the water carefully at your put-in, your take-out, and at as many points in between as possible before launching. Probably the best way to tell when a river is running at high-water stage is by checking the shoreline. If trees and bushes are standing in water, the river is above normal. Consequently, a trip on it may vary considerably from my description. Conversely, when the shoreline vegetation is some distance from the water, the river is abnormally low. This situation can cause another set of problems. You may run aground or get hung up on rocks, and spend as much time walking your canoe as paddling.

Dams and water releases also play a major role in fluctuating water levels on the rivers. The fastest-moving rivers in particular are subject to great variations in the amount of water being released, which in turn depends upon power requirements. As a general rule, more water is released on weekdays than on weekends, with the smallest flowage usually on Sundays, when power requirements are smallest. Major power companies often can supply you with a schedule of water releases on the larger rivers.

I've tried to indicate which rivers can be run through the drier summer months and which are strictly spring rivers. All the white-water trips are best made long before summer arrives because the rivers all become extremely shallow later in the season. On the whitewater runs, I have chosen sections that are exciting and scenic but have omitted the more dangerous stretches. I have used the same ratings for the rapids on these runs as used by the American Canoe Association, the Appalachian Mountain Club, and most other prominent canoeing organizations.

In these ratings, Class I is moving water with some riffles, small waves, and few or no obstacles. Class II indicates small-scale rapids where there are wide channels that are obvious without scouting from shore. Class III rapids should be scouted—they are capable of swamping canoes. They have high, irregular waves that arise from water running through narrow, twisting passages. Only a few of the rivers in this book—the upper Farmington, the Shepaug, the Salmon, and possibly the faster stretch of the Housatonic or part of the Deerfield—generate Class III rapids, and then only under abnormal conditiions. Class IV and Class V rapids are for expert canoeists only; therefore no river trips that would involve such sections have been included.

Larry Millard, the photographer, and I spent nearly two years canoeing the rivers of southern New England to make these 25 selections. We drove approximately 5,000 miles and checked out

Wetsuits and life preservers are musts on whitewater trips in early spring; this team skillfully negotiates a rough patch on the Moosup.

You are likely to meet fishermen on many of southern New England's rivers; this angler plays a fish on the Willimantic.

every part of the three states we cover. We canoed hundreds of miles. Larry is a life-long resident of New England, and I am a transplanted Ohioan, but we continually found ourselves expressing the same opinions. These rivers are beautiful, much more so than most people would believe possible in such heavily populated, "civilized" states as Massachusetts, Connecticut, and Rhode Island. We discovered a fortune in canoeing enjoyment. I hope you will agree.

Ken Weber

Summary of Canoeing Terms

Most technical canoeing terms were omitted from this book so beginning canoeists would find the descriptions relatively easy to understand. The following terms, however, are used. Knowing their meanings will make your reading more enjoyable and your canoeing safer.

Back eddy: The water immediately downstream from a boulder or other obstruction. The water is forced to swirl around the obstruction and flow momentarily upstream. These eddies are valuable on fast-moving rivers because you can use them for rest breaks or to check on following canoes.

Back watering: The process of paddling backward, that is, against the current; a technique often used in fast water and rapids to slow down, turn, or stop.

Blowdown: A fallen tree in the river, usually at least partially blocking the canoe's path.

Bottom scrapers: The term commonly used to describe rocks just below the water's surface.

Bow: The front end of a canoe.

Carry: Another word for portage; an obstacle (usually a dam) that cannot be canoed over or around. The canoe must be taken out of the water, carried around the obstacle, and launched again.

Channel: The route through the riverbed that carries the deepest water and the strongest currents.

Chute: A break in a ledge or dam that acts as a funnel for the water. Chutes are often, but not always, canoeable.

Current: The rate of flow in a river. Strong current means the water is moving very fast.

Deadwater: Refers to water that is not moving; usually associated with water just above a dam.

Downstream: The direction in which the water is flowing.

Draw stroke: A valuable technique in whitewater canoeing; refers to reaching out to the side of the canoe, plunging the paddle into the water, and pulling or drawing the paddle toward you. This, in effect, moves the canoe in the direction of your paddle. It is used to make quick, sharp maneuvers.

Eddy: The quiet water behind obstacles. Eddies are often used for taking rest breaks.

Flatwater: Refers to water, whether moving or still, that shows no signs of turbulence.

Headwind: Any wind blowing in the faces of the canoeists; a major problem when canoeing large ponds or very wide rivers.

Hung up: A term canoeists use for running aground on a sandbar or, more often, for being immobilized atop a rock in shallow water.

Landing: A spot on the shore from which canoes can easily be put in or taken out of the water.

Launching: The act of putting a canoe in the water.

Liftover: An obstacle, usually a fallen tree or log. It is passed by floating up to it, stepping out, and lifting the canoe over it.

Lining: A method of taking the canoe through extremely shallow water. Canoeists walk in the water or along the shore while allowing the empty canoe to float and keep control of the canoe by means of an attached rope or line.

Low water: Refers to a river's condition when the water level is unusually low; a situation common in summer and autumn.

Meander: A winding path; refers to rivers that curl back and forth in a wandering pattern.

Passage: A route or path; used in canoeing to refer to the way around an obstacle, such as the right or left passage around an island.

Portage: As a noun, refers to an impassable obstacle in the river; as a verb, refers to the act of taking the canoe out of the water, carrying it around the obstacle, and putting it back in the water.

Put-in: The spot from which you launch your canoe and begin a trip.

Quickwater: Refers to fast-moving water with some turbulence; not as severe as rapids or whitewater.

Rapids: Water cascading over rocks with the water flowing very fast and the rocks large enough and close enough together to create a roaring, sometimes dangerous turbulence.

Riffles: Water flowing over small rocks causing only minor turbulence or a "bumpy" surface.

Rock dodging: Refers to maneuvering a canoe between rocks or boulders in the riverbed.

Scouting: Checking the water ahead, usually from shore; a prudent practice prior to canoeing rapids to decide which route to take.

Scratchy: Refers to rivers so shallow the canoe is likely to scrape rocks on the bottom, or be scratched, in passing.

Standing waves: Whitecapped waves of turbulent water caused by water pouring over a dam, boulder, or some other obstacle.

Stern: The back end of the canoe.

Swamping: Also sometimes called dumping; refers to the canoe being filled with water.

Take-out: The end of your trip; where you take the canoe out of the water.

Tides: The movement of ocean waters to land, or up rivers, and out again; in this book applicable only on the saltwater trips: Osterville-Grand Island, the North River, and the Pettaquamscutt (Narrow) River.

Upstream: The direction from which the water is flowing.

Wetsuit: A heavy rubber suit worn next to the skin for warmth when canoeing wild rivers in cold weather.

Whitewater: Refers to rivers on which the water flows over and around rocks with so much force that it creates a white foam.

Trips in
Massachusetts

1

Deerfield River
Below Shelburne Falls to Greenfield

Put-in Point	Take-out Points	Approximate Distance	Approximate Trip Time	Condition of Water	Portages
Bardwell Ferry Road bridge	I-91 bridges	4 miles	1½ hours	Riffles	None
Bardwell Ferry Road bridge	US 5-MA 10 bridge	10¼ miles	3-3½ hours	Riffles, then mostly smooth	None

Timing is all important when planning a canoeing trip on the Deerfield River in northwestern Massachusetts. The Deerfield is a river of many moods. At times it is a crashing, churning, terrifying waterway. And at other times, and in stretches only a few miles away from the whitewater, the river can be so sedate, so serene you'll wonder if the water is moving at all. If you catch the Deerfield between these two extremes, you will experience one of the easiest and yet most rewarding trips in southern New England. Do the 10¼-mile segment described here just after high water, but before the river drops to its summer level and you will be treated to a delightful 3½-hour float that begins amid ledges and forests and ends in a farmland valley.

This trip starts at the Bardwell Ferry Road bridge below the town of Shelburne Falls and finishes beside the US 5-MA 10 bridge near Greenfield. Some whitewater canoeists run another section of the upper Deerfield above Charlemont but that area, which includes the notorious Zoar Gap, is extremely dangerous, especially in springtime. Several lives have been lost there in recent years. It is definitely not recommended.

Although there are no dams on the section of the Deerfield described here, there are several upriver at Shelburne Falls that will affect your canoeing. They combine with the hilly terrain in varying the flow of water considerably. The water level rises and drops

Ledges and rock outcroppings alternate with dense forest on the Deerfield just below the Bardwell Ferry Road bridge.

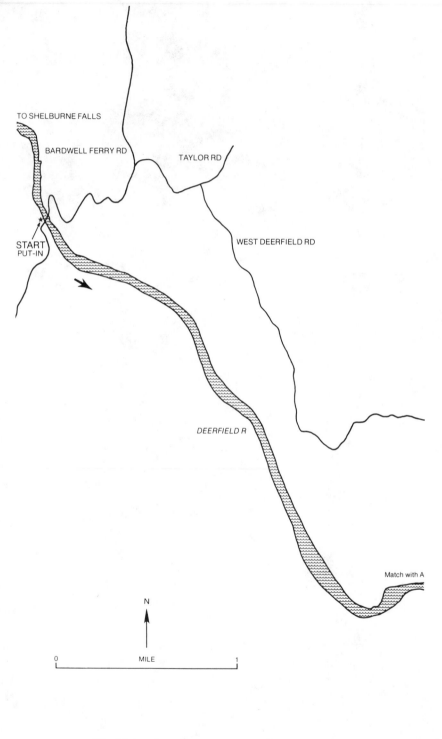

TO SHELBURNE FALLS

BARDWELL FERRY RD

TAYLOR RD

WEST DEERFIELD RD

START
PUT-IN

DEERFIELD R

Match with A

N

0　　　　　　　　　　MILE　　　　　　　　　　1

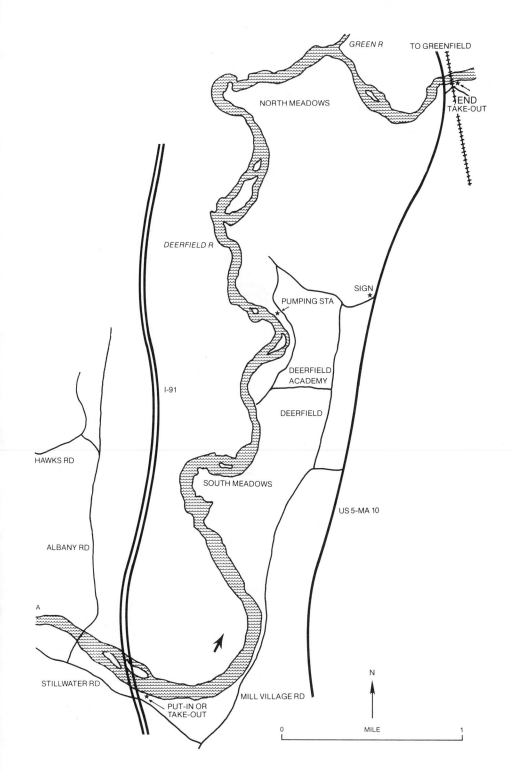

GREEN R

TO GREENFIELD

NORTH MEADOWS

END
TAKE-OUT

DEERFIELD R

SIGN

PUMPING STA

DEERFIELD
ACADEMY

DEERFIELD

I-91

HAWKS RD

SOUTH MEADOWS

US 5-MA 10

ALBANY RD

A

STILLWATER RD

MILL VILLAGE RD

PUT-IN OR
TAKE-OUT

N

0   MILE   1

23   *Massachusetts*

quickly; to catch it at its best, go just a few days after sudden thaws or heavy rains. We once canoed this stretch under ideal conditions— there was enough water so that we floated over rocks, a steady current, and no dangers. One week earlier, however, the river had been in flood stage. During that week, the water level dropped eight feet.

Access

To leave a car at the take-out point, drive US 5-MA 10 to where it crosses the river just south of Greenfield. There is a small parking area on a side road on the south end of the bridge, just beyond a railroad bridge that parallels the highway bridge.

Now haul your canoe to the starting point by following US 5-MA 10 south to the sign indicating "Historic Deerfield" on the right. Drive through this colonial-era village, past Deerfield Academy, and you will come to Mill Village Road, which takes you back to the river. Turn right on Stillwater Road, pass under I-91 (an alternate put-in/take-out), turn right again on Albany Road, and cross the river. Now the driving adventure begins. One mile past the bridge Hawks Road angles off to the left. Follow this narrow and winding hill road until it runs into Taylor Road in 2½ miles (here Hawks Road is called West Deerfield Road). Turn left onto Taylor Road and then left again at Bardwell Ferry Road. In another mile of switchback driving you'll arrive at the put-in. Park just beyond the high bridge.

At the right rear corner of the parking area, which is often filled on weekends with the cars of fishermen, you'll find a path leading down to some large flat rocks almost under the bridge. Launching a canoe here is quite easy. There are lots of riffles just upstream, but it is usually relatively smooth beneath the bridge. There will be enough current, however, to help you along your way immediately.

The River

Start/
Bardwell
Ferry Road
bridge

This first stretch may be the prettiest of your trip. Certainly it provides the greatest feeling of wilderness. Ledges and rock outcroppings are scattered about on both shores, alternating with stands of dense forest. Numerous little brooks cascade down the rocky slopes in early spring and after heavy rains. You may even get lucky—as we did—and spot a beaver swimming by. There are several colonies in the area, although the beaver usually remain in the smaller streams.

You will come to the first set of riffles quickly, but when there is enough water they are no problem. Nor are most of the others that have to be negotiated at brief intervals. In low water, the riffles are bottom scrapers or worse. But if you go at the recommended time—when the river is slightly high—they are just fun. You will zoom right over the rocks in a fast current. Only a few spots are wild enough to be considered more than riffles, and they are no more than Class I rapids in the American Canoe Association rating system. The river is wide and pretty all the way, and as you progress there are more smooth stretches than riffly ones. Sandbars jut out from the shores and combine with boulders and ledges to provide many inviting spots for resting, fishing, or picture taking.

You should reach the Albany Road bridge in about an hour. The next set of bridges, the double I-91 crossings, are just a short distance farther, past one more lengthy riffle. If you elect to take out here, swing to the right under the second bridge. Beyond I-91 the river runs through farmland, passes through an area called South Meadows, swings around the town of Deerfield, and meanders through North Meadows on the way to your take-out. There are several shallow spots where the river runs around gravel bars in the first mile or so past I-91, but the current remains strong and finding the main channel is not difficult.

I-91 bridges

You will get only an occasional glimpse of buildings in Deerfield as you pass the village. You can tie up and walk into the town, however, when you reach a brick pumping station on your right. There is a road here, behind Deerfield Academy, but it is not a good alternate take-out because the slope is steep and covered with jagged stones.

The remaining 3 miles from Deerfield to the US 5-MA 10 bridge are very smooth and relaxing. The river flows slightly deeper and divides around a string of islands. Most are wooded, but one is a huge red rock that looks out of place. It would seem more appropriate in some Arizona or New Mexico river. Although trees continue to line the banks, the setting is obviously pastoral. You may see herds of cattle drowsing in the shade or hear tractors being worked in the nearby fields. Still, the banks obscure and muffle most of the distractions, and the river's soothing character produces an idyllic charm.

When you reach the Green River coming in from the left, itself a tranquil little stream here after tumultuous beginnings farther north, you are nearing the end of your trip. The take-out point is very easy to find. In addition to the highway and railroad bridges you float under, look for concrete pillars and stone abutments left from long-vanished structures. Pull out on the right, just beyond the railroad bridge.

US 5-MA 10 bridge/end

Ware River

Ware to Thorndike

Put-in Points	Take-out Points	Approximate Distance	Approximate Trip Time	Condition of Water	Portages
Farm lane south of Ware	State Street bridge	5½ miles	2 hours	Some riffles, some smooth	None
Farm lane south of Ware	Thorndike Dam	6⅔ miles	2½-3 hours	Some riffles, last part smooth	None
MA 32 bridge	State Street bridge	3¾ miles	1½ hours	Mostly smooth	None
MA 32 bridge	Thorndike Dam	5 miles	2-2½ hours	Mostly smoth	None

The Ware River, northeast of Springfield in central Massachusetts, can be a little gem. Rarely used by canoeists, the Ware offers several miles of casual floating through forests and farmland. I say it "can be" a gem because like most rivers the Ware is subject to changing conditions; the water can be extremely low and scratchy during summer and is occasionally discolored from effluent dumped by the mills upriver. Most of the time, however, the Ware is the kind of waterway canoeists look for when they want to spend just a few hours on an easy, relaxed cruise.

The total length of the segment described here, which runs from about 1½ miles south of downtown Ware to a dam in the village of Thorndike, is only 6⅔ miles. This stretch normally can be canoed in 2½ to 3 hours, even with a lunch break. Most of the few riffles you will encounter are within the first couple of miles. Thus, the MA 32 bridge provides an excellent alternate put-in for those who want flatwater only. And if the water just above the take-out at Thorndike Dam is too smooth and still for your taste, there is a handy alternate take-out at the State Street bridge a little more than a mile upriver. You can choose just what you want on this river.

Trees give way to grassy fields as you come down to the State Street bridge take-out, just visible as you round the bend.

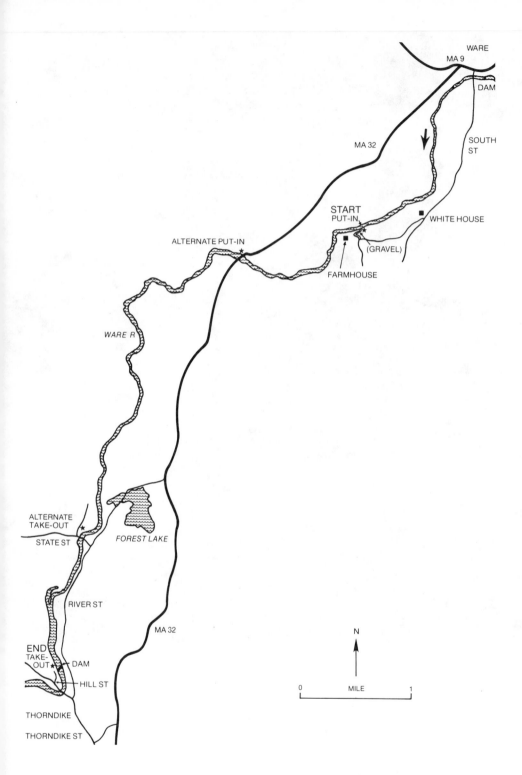

WARE
MA 9
DAM

MA 32

SOUTH
ST

START
PUT-IN

WHITE HOUSE

ALTERNATE PUT-IN

(GRAVEL)

FARMHOUSE

WARE R

ALTERNATE
TAKE-OUT

STATE ST

FOREST LAKE

RIVER ST

MA 32

N

END
TAKE-
OUT

DAM

HILL ST

0   MILE   1

THORNDIKE

THORNDIKE ST

28 *Massachusetts*

Access

If you are planning to paddle the full distance, you will want to leave a car at the Thorndike Dam take-out. Follow MA 32 to Thorndike Street, which you will take into the village, past River Street, and across the river. Turn right on Hill Street and drive to the dam, where there is room to park several cars.

To reach the put-in, you can take MA 32 north to Ware, or you can follow River Street, which runs along the east side of the river. This street not only provides several good views of the water you will be canoeing, it also brings you to State Street, where there is an alternate take-out. River Street then rejoins MA 32, which in a few miles more crosses the river again, where there is still another possible put-in/take-out point.

Continuing on MA 32 all the way into Ware, turn right on South Street (beyond the junction of MA 32 and MA 9) at a corner next to the Ware Cooperative Bank. Almost immediately you will cross the river one more time, just below a dam, but there is too little water here to canoe, so take a reading on your odometer and continue on South Street until you have driven $1\frac{1}{2}$ miles south from the MA 32/MA 9 turnoff. This will bring you to a white house beyond which a side road angles off to the right. Follow this road as it winds downhill. As it nears the river, the road curves left, but a paved lane continues ahead and then breaks right near a farm. Stay with the lane. It crosses an old railroad track and then ends at a field entrance near the river. Park beside the lane, taking care not to block the path. Recent removal of several trees has made it easier to carry your gear down the slope and then to launch your canoe.

The River

Start/
Farm lane

Putting in here instead of at the more convenient MA 32 landing adds only about 1½ miles to your trip, but it can be worth the extra effort. When there is enough water—usually through early June—this section can be fast and fun without being dangerous. There are no major rapids, but numerous stretches of riffles will require some care and skill. In low water, you'll scrape bottom in several of the patches of rocks, but in higher water you'll have a pleasant float that will carry you to the MA 32 bridge in about half an hour.

MA 32
bridge

Just beyond the MA 32 bridge, there is a shallow, riffly area, then you begin floating into smooth stretches. There are still some gentle riffles, but for the most part the water is smooth enough to allow you to sit back and enjoy the scenery. This segment—MA 32 to State Street—is just under 4 miles long and is probably the most attractive stretch of the trip. At first, there are good forests on both sides, with occasional hemlocks and pines appearing among the dominant maples, birches, and oaks. Kingbirds and swallows play tag over the water, orioles sing from the treetops, and ducks squawk off in protest as you silently float around the bends. Once in a while, you'll see something less common in this area, too, perhaps an otter or a great horned owl. We have.

As you pass a grassy island—you can take either passage—the shorelines open into picturesque pastures. These expanses of green grass lead off to distant barns and houses framed by the hills along the horizon. There are still a few big trees at the water's edge here, mostly majestic oaks; they invite you ashore for a picnic break. Eventually, however, the forested banks return. Then, shortly after you float under a railroad bridge you will notice a string of cottages on the left, just back from the bank. The houses face a small lake; the river is in their backyards.

In a few minutes more the right shore flattens out again and the trees give way to grass once more. Soon the State Street bridge comes into view. If this is your take-out, swing over to the right and and pull out just before the bridge. Those planning to finish at Thorndike have another 1½ miles of mirror-smooth paddling.

State Street

Beyond State Street, you will quickly begin to feel the effects of the Thorndike Dam, for the current practically disappears. Still, this extra hour on the water is pleasant. There are several houses on the left, but tall trees line both sides. This smooth paddle is an enjoyable way to cap the day. The take-out, at the right end of the dam, is easy, just the way this trip should be concluded.

Thorndike Dam/end

Quaboag River

Brookfield to Warren

Put-in Points	Take-out Point	Approximate Distance	Approximate Trip Time	Condition of Water	Portages
MA 148 bridge	Lucy Stone Park	6¾ miles	2½-3 hours	Smooth	None
MA 67 bridge	Lucy Stone Park	2½ miles	1 hour	Smooth	None

The Quaboag River in south central Massachusetts is something of a "backward" river. Other rivers, particularly those in hilly country such as central and western Massachusetts, begin small and fast and eventually grow wider and slower. Not the Quaboag. This river is full grown at birth, a broad, languid stream meandering through marshland. Farther along, the Quaboag turns into a tumbling white-water river.

Only experts should run the Quaboag rapids, which extend from Warren to Blanchardville, east of Springfield. But anyone who knows which end of a paddle to hold can do this trip on the upper Quaboag. Here the river is wide, smooth and easy, with only the wind as a possible drawback. A strong breeze from the west or northwest can make you work hard in the first section of this trip, for the river is mostly open water with little protection from the elements.

At all other times, canoeing the upper Quaboag is a most pleasant way for family groups or beginners to spend a few hours. The river wanders through a marsh rich in wildlife and aquatic plants, and then narrows somewhat as it enters woodlands. Finally, it picks up speed as it bubbles past a few minor riffles shortly before the take-out. The full distance of the trip is about 6¾ miles; it can usually be canoed in 2½ to 3 hours.

Access

Take-out will be in Warren, at Lucy Stone Park, a small parking area beside a bridge on River Street (called Old West Brookfield Road outside the village of Warren), just upriver from the main part of the

Views are expansive in the marshy stretch of the Quaboag.

town. The park is on the west side of the road, at the spot where the river bends and then plunges into the first set of rapids. For those not familiar with quickwater techniques, the preferred take-out is just before the bridge on the left bank. Pulling out here and carrying your canoe across the road to your car is easier and safer than trying to combat the swift currents and rocks beyond the bridge.

To reach the put-in, return to Warren and take MA 67 north to MA 9, or drive north on Old West Brookfield Road, which changes into Old Warren Road, until it meets MA 9. You can put in here where MA 67 crosses the river, at a spot popular with fishermen. If you launch here, however, the distance to the bridge by Lucy Stone Park is only about 2½ miles—perhaps 1 hour on the water. Therefore, it is better to continue on MA 9 east through West Brookfield to MA 148 in Brookfield. Turn right on MA 148 and drive to the river. You will find good access on the left, just before the bridge.

The River

Start/
MA 148
bridge

The MA 148 access is just west of Quaboag Pond, which is fed by smaller streams and in turn forms the Quaboag River. Because of this pond, nearby Wickaboag Pond, and other large ponds in its watershed, the Quaboag usually has plenty of water and can be canoed easily most of the year. The current and depth vary far less than in most rivers.

The best time to begin this trip is usually early morning, before the wind springs up and while the wildlife is still active. You are likely to spot great blue herons prowling the eelgrass and pickerel-weeds on both sides of the river, as well as green herons, ducks of several varieties, and maybe even bitterns or rails—shy, elusive birds seldom seen away from marshes and certainly not seen by canoeists shooting rapids. Muskrats are found here, too, and occasionally the early riser can glimpse a mink or otter.

Little can be seen of the towns on the right as you move downriver, for the buildings are screened from view by trees. On the left a series of hills makes up the horizon. By the time you reach the first bridge, an iron span at West Brookfield, the river is beginning to narrow slightly, but it retains its marshy atmosphere

MA 67
bridge

until just beyond the MA 67 bridge, approximately 4¼ miles from your start. Here the river curves to the left, and for the first time flows close to the trees. Look to the right, especially if you are weary of paddling through marshes, and you will be able to gauge your progress. Painted on a red shed in the woods is a white arrow pointing downriver and the words, "To Warren, 2 Mi."

In just a few minutes, you will leave the trees and return to paddling in an open marsh. As the banks fall away, you will be presented with good views of the hillsides and some of the area's alluring old farms—weathered buildings, lush meadows, and miles

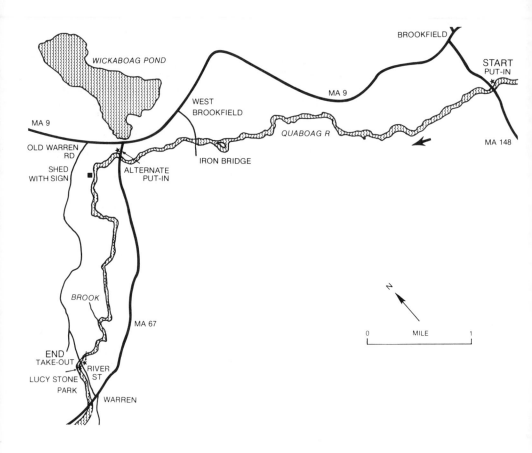

of stone walls. Those rocky slopes may be hard to plow, but they are certainly appealing to the passerby.

This swampy section belongs to red-winged blackbirds and swallows, but the bird population changes as the river narrows and re-enters the woods. Orioles, kingfishers, and vireos can be seen in the overhead branches, and warblers and wrens seem to follow along with you in the undergrowth on the shores.

Look for a brook that adds to the current joining the river from the right. Soon you will see a few boulders scattered about. There are no rapids, but occasionally you will encounter brief riffles, all easy to handle. The Quaboag is a forest river now, with tall birches, maples, and oaks, high banks complete with muskrat slides, and a

34 *Massachusetts*

steady current. Little effort beyond steering around the numerous bends is required in this area.

When you come abreast of several large boulders on a point reaching out from the left, you are nearing your trip's end. Just beyond the point, you will see the back of a large wooden sign that identifies a nature trail installed here by the Warren Conservation Commission. By now, the River Street-Old West Brookfield Road bridge is in view. Swing to the left shore and take out before reaching the bridge. If you go under the bridge, you might get a taste of the "other" Quaboag—tumbling whitewater—whether you want to or not.

Lucy
Stone
Park/end

Concord River
Concord to Billerica

Put-in Point	Take-out Points	Approximate Distance	Approximate Trip Time	Condition of Water	Portages
Lowell Road access	MA 225 bridge	4¼ miles	2 hours	Smooth	None
Lowell Road access	MA 4 bridge	6¼ miles	3 hours	Smooth	None
Lowell Road access	River Street bridge	8½ miles	4-4½ hours	Smooth	None
Lowell Road access	MA 3A bridge	10 miles	4½-5 hours	Smooth	None

"I have often stood on the banks of the Concord, watching the lapse of the current, an emblem of all progress, following the same law with the system, with time, and all that is made; the weeds at the bottom gently bending down the stream, shaken by the watery wind, still planted where their seeds had sunk, but ere long to die and go down likewise; the shining pebbles, not yet anxious to better their condition, the chips and weeds, and occasional logs and stems of trees that floated past, fulfilling their fate, were objects of singular interest to me, and at last I resolved to launch myself on its bosom, and float whither it would bear me."

So wrote Henry David Thoreau in 1839 in his book *A Week on the Concord and Merrimack Rivers*. While launching yourself on the Concord today and floating whither it bears you may not inspire the poetry and philosophy that it did for Thoreau, the river remains among the best waterways in northeastern Massachusetts for relaxed canoe touring. From Concord to Billerica, you will find 10 miles of smooth water with no portages, plenty of attractive shoreline scenery, and a great deal of history.

Early in your trip you will pass beneath a replica of the Old North

*Pull out on the right bank just below the wooden bridge for a brief stroll
through Minute Man National Historic Park.*

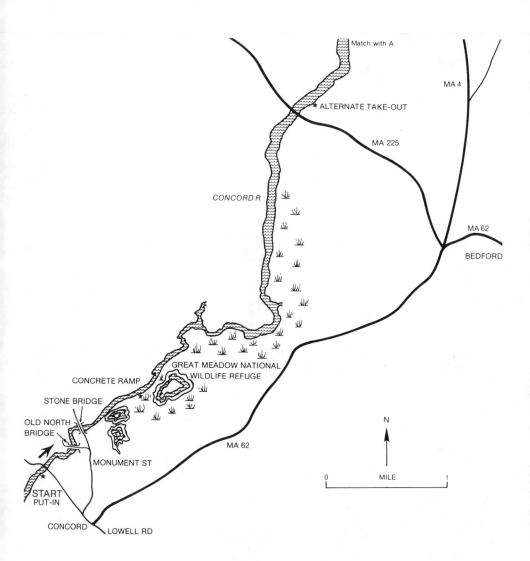

Bridge, where the first shots of the Revolutionary War were fired. The hillsides of this area, now silent and serene, ran out in 1775 with the call to arms of the "embattled farmers." It takes only a little knowledge of those events to make a cruise down the Concord River something special.

I recommend making this trip in autumn rather than summer, for

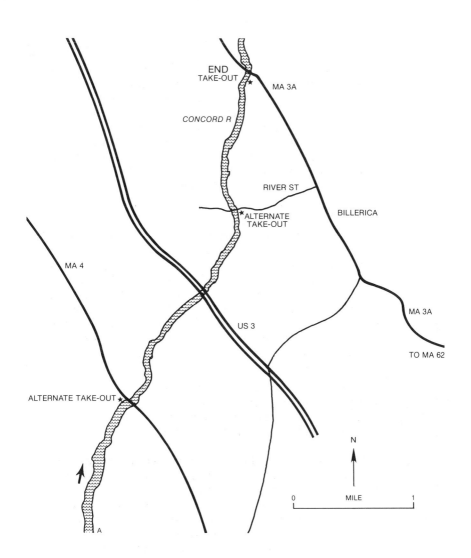

the Concord is often crowded with powerboats during the warmer months, particularly on weekends. Moreover, in autumn you will reap the full benefit of the foliage, and get to enjoy the ducks and geese that flock to a wildlife refuge that flanks a long section of your journey. Also, you will be more closely following Thoreau's adventure, for he made his trip by rowboat in September.

Access

This trip can be shortened very easily, with excellent access for take-outs available at the MA 225 bridge (about 4¼ miles from Concord), the MA 4 bridge (6½ miles), or at River Street in Billerica (8½ miles). For the full 10 miles, however, leave a car next to the bridge on MA 3A north of Billerica. Then, to haul your canoe to put-in, drive south 5 miles to MA 62, turn right and continue all the way to Concord, about 10 miles. By the Colonial Inn, turn right onto Lowell Road and travel just beyond the village to the river. A public access lane is on the left, just before the bridge.

The River

Start/
Lowell
Road
access

Just minutes after launching at the Lowell Road bridge, you will reach the site of the historic skirmish of April 19, 1775. A wooden bridge, built on the order of the original, arches over the water. Often this bridge is crowded with tourists, for it is located in the Minute Man National Historic Park. Float under the bridge, and then pull out on the right for a brief stroll. It is worth the time and effort. You will find markers commemorating the British soldiers who fell that day on the right side of the river. Cross the bridge for a look at the Minute Man statue and its inscription from the famous Longfellow poem:

> "By the rude bridge that arched the flood,
> Their flag to April's breeze unfurled,
> Here once the embattled farmers stood,
> And fired the shot heard 'round the world."

Back on the river, you soon come to another picturesque bridge, this one made of stone. From this point it is calm and peaceful paddling for some distance between wooded banks, with silver maples the dominant trees. Fields stretch away beyond the trees on the left while the sprawling Great Meadows National Wildlife Refuge takes in most of the land beside the river on the right. When you begin seeing the refuge signs, look for a concrete ramp on the right. You can pull out here, walk inland for a few yards to a bench, and with binoculars scan a protected marsh where waterfowl congregate in autumn. Often you will hear far more geese and ducks than you can see, the gabbling, a true song of fall, accompanying you for several miles down the river.

Soon you will leave the tall trees and high banks behind and move into an open, swampy area where the river widens and bushes are the primary vegetation. You will now be able to see numerous fine homes guarded by stately groves of pines on the hills to the left.

MA 225
bridge

At the next bridge, MA 225, there is a public landing site on the right. Boating activity in this area and over the next few miles can be heavy. The river is open and easy from here for the 2 miles to

MA 4 bridge — the MA 4 bridge, where there is a marina and another concrete ramp. The stretch of river just beyond MA 4 passes numerous homes, most of which are equipped with boats, ramps, piers, and little beaches. After this segment, the river narrows and becomes more attractive as you pass the double bridges for US 3 (no access). Oaks and maples, resplendent in autumn, crowd the banks, and you are likely to flush herons and sandpipers, as well as ducks, as you paddle around the bends.

River Street bridge —

MA 3A bridge/end —

It takes about an hour to complete the trip from the US 3 bridges, past the nearby River Street bridge, where a take-out is possible on the right, to your planned terminus just before the MA 3A bridge on the left. Houses line this last stretch on the left side and then you will see the businesses on MA 3A. A number of fast-food restaurants will emphasize your return to the present. Thoreau also ended his first day's journey near here, but he dined that night on wild huckleberries.

Shawsheen River
Billerica to Ballardvale

Put-In Point	Take-Out Points	Approximate Distance	Approximate Trip Time	Condition of Water	Portages
MA 3A bridge	MA 129 bridge	3 miles	1½ hours	Smooth	Liftovers
MA 3A bridge	MA 38 bridge	5 miles	2½ hours	Smooth, then some quick-water	Liftovers
MA 3A bridge	Ballardvale bridge	10 miles	4½-5 hours	Smooth, some quickwater, then mostly smooth	Liftovers

The Indians knew what they were doing when they named this river the Shawsheen. The word means "serpentine, to meander." The Shawsheen certainly meanders, winding back and forth in a seemingly endless series of switchbacks, hairpins, and half circles. Still, it is a pleasant little river to canoe, particularly for somebody in no hurry at all. You can't rush down the Shawsheen. If you try, the river's tendency to "go three times around the house to get to the barn" will be maddening. No, the way to enjoy the Shawsheen is to give yourself a full day, take a lunch, float and paddle at a leisurely pace, and forget all about the clock. Under these conditions, the river can be a joy.

The Shawsheen, a mere squiggle on most maps, runs northeasterly between Boston and Lowell and eventually empties into the Merrimack River. The best stretch for canoeing is the 10 miles from the MA 3A bridge south of Billerica to the village of Ballardvale, south of Andover. Shorter trips too are easily arranged, with access points at the MA 129 and MA 38 bridges. The MA 129 bridge is about 3 miles, water distance, from MA 3A and the bridge at MA 38 is at the 5-mile mark, about midway to the take-out at Ballardvale.

A word of caution. Do not attempt this river late in the year or during periods of extremely low water. We did it once in September, and what is normally a 4½- or 5-hour float took about 7 hours.

Looking upstream at the stone bridge and relics of a long-gone canal—in low water it would be wise to line your canoe through here.

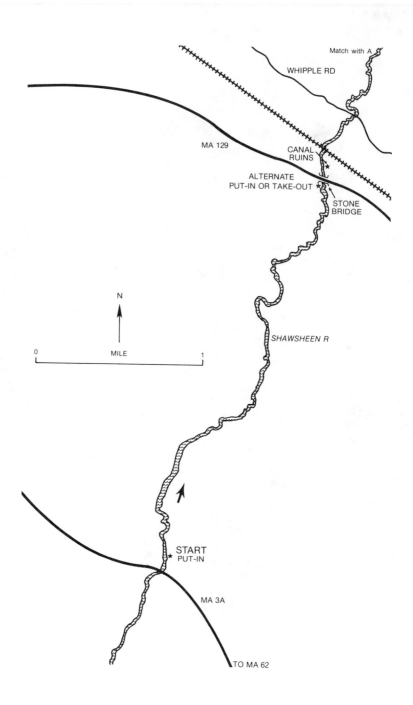

Match with A

WHIPPLE RD

MA 129

CANAL
RUINS

ALTERNATE
PUT-IN OR TAKE-OUT

STONE
BRIDGE

N

0   MILE   1

SHAWSHEEN R

START
PUT-IN

MA 3A

TO MA 62

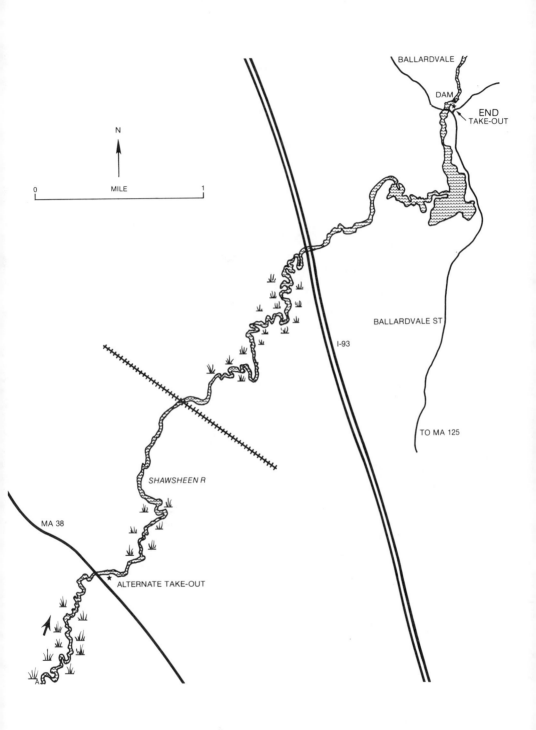

N

0   MILE   1

BALLARDVALE

DAM

END
TAKE-OUT

BALLARDVALE ST

I-93

TO MA 125

SHAWSHEEN R

MA 38

ALTERNATE TAKE-OUT

Moreover, there was more lining and lifting than most canoeists care to undertake.

With enough water, however, the river is relatively easy to negotiate. There is a steady current throughout most of the trip, with a dash of quickwater at the middle. Then comes a paddle through a quiet millpond above Ballardvale and finally the take-out. Along the way, you will alternate between woodsy settings and open marshes where the river's meandering takes place. At times, you will float behind strings of houses; moments later you will be following the curves through what looks like a primeval swamp.

Access

To canoe the full 10 miles, take I-93 to MA 125 north. Take first left, Ballardvale Street, off MA 125 and follow that street into the village. A bridge just above a dam is your destination. Take a narrow side street to the right just before the bridge and park beneath a string of willow trees near the Shawsheen Rubber Company. Leaving one car here, drive back to MA 125, take I-93 south and then turn onto MA 62 west. Drive through Wilmington on MA 62, turn right (north) on MA 3A, and continue to the bridge over the river. The bridge is just beyond Pinehurst Park, an office complex, on the right. A parking lot extends to the water and there is room to leave a car here as well. The distance by car from Ballardvale is 12 miles.

The River

Start/
MA 3A
bridge

The first stretch beyond the put-in at MA 3A is very narrow, a ribbon of water snaking between grassy banks. Soon, however, you will enter the woods. Here the river widens slightly, and there is good water depth. You may encounter fallen trees and snags that require liftovers, and there is one wooden footbridge behind a group of houses that is too low to pass beneath. However, in most of the swampy areas, where you do little more than turn and then turn again, the channel is usually clear and deep enough.

MA 129
bridge

In 3 miles, you reach the MA 129 bridge. As mentioned, you can take out here. However, one of the most enjoyable stretches of the river lies just ahead. If you are going on, pass under the stone bridge, keeping to the far right, and then maneuver by the large stones in the river just beyond. These are relics of the abutments built for a long-vanished canal. A high column of stone still stands in the middle of the river and you should use care in passing it. When the water is high, you can float by, but in shallow water it would be wise to swing across the current and go to the left of the column. There are times when you may have to line your canoe through here.

You then pass a railroad bridge, with abutments also made of stone, and return to paddling between wooded shores. Once again, the river is quite narrow and consequently subject to blowdown problems on occasion. Fallen trees sometimes catch on the opposite shore, causing a barrier that traps branches and debris floating downriver. Most of these you can get through with only a few liftovers. After passing a small bridge you will return to the marshes and the meandering route. Then, about 2 miles from MA 129, you will reach the MA 38 bridge. You can take out here on the right just beyond the bridge if you have decided on a shorter trip.

MA 38 bridge

The last half of this run has more of the outstanding features of the first half, but in larger doses. For quickwater, there is a rapid rated as Class II by the American Canoe Association. When we went in September, the water was so shallow we had to walk, but in spring running this rapid is exciting and fun. For small bridges, there is one that resembles a double culvert, with the right side, which carries more water, looking as if it is about to collapse. For natural attractions, there is a section of fine tall pines, oaks, and maples standing guard over the river. And for meandering waterways, there are dozens of hairpin turns that nearly have you meeting yourself over and over again in the area just before the I-93 bridge. You can hear the traffic and see the bridge perhaps half an hour before you finally reach it.

Once past the I-93 bridges (no access), you have only about 2 miles left to paddle. The first mile is through an attractive wooded area that would be even more attractive were it not for a factory and its discharges into the water. The second mile of this final segment is through a long pond created by the dam at Ballardvale. This is a deadwater stretch with little or no current. You will have to be careful not to wander off into backwaters that go nowhere. Tall weeds and rushes grow here, helping to make this area a gathering place for ducks and shorebirds, but the lush vegetation can make the main channel difficult to find. For the most part, if you keep bearing left when in doubt you'll be able to follow the channel. Immediately after passing under the bridge before the dam, swing to the right for take-out.

Ballardvale bridge/ end

Ipswich River
Topsfield

Put-In Point	Take-Out Points	Approximate Distance	Approximate Trip Time	Condition of Water	Portages
MA 97 bridge	Asbury Street bridge	6 Miles	2½-3 hours	Smooth	None
MA 97 bridge	Ipswich Road	7 miles	3-3½ hours	Smooth	None

One of the more popular canoeing rivers in eastern Massachusetts, the Ipswich is like a fine wine or a good book. It should never be hurried through, but tasted and savored a little bit at a time. Pause often and absorb the atmosphere. It can be most rewarding. The stretch described here runs through Wenham Swamp southeast of Topsfield. This is the most intriguing portion of the river, and the part most easily canoed at any time of the year. During high-water periods you can continue all the way downriver into the village of Ipswich. The last several miles, however, are impassable during much of the summer and autumn. This lower section also includes two portages and—when there is any water at all—stretches of fast water.

From the MA 97 bridge to Ipswich Road, however, you'll have no portages and all smooth water. The total distance, snaking through the vast swamp, is approximately 7 miles, although you can shorten the trip slightly by taking out at the Asbury Street bridge. Canoeing at a leisurely pace, the paddle to Asbury Street takes only about 3 hours, and it's just a few minutes more to Ipswich Road.

Unlike many swamps, which resemble weedy millponds, Wenham swamp is liberally sprinkled with vibrant stands of trees, many perched on attractive islands and knolls. Even when you're out in the most wide open parts of the swamp, you'll never be far from a wooded retreat. The fascination of swamp life, however, is there.

Woodland Siamese twins reach for the water—just one of several fascinating sights in Wenham Swamp.

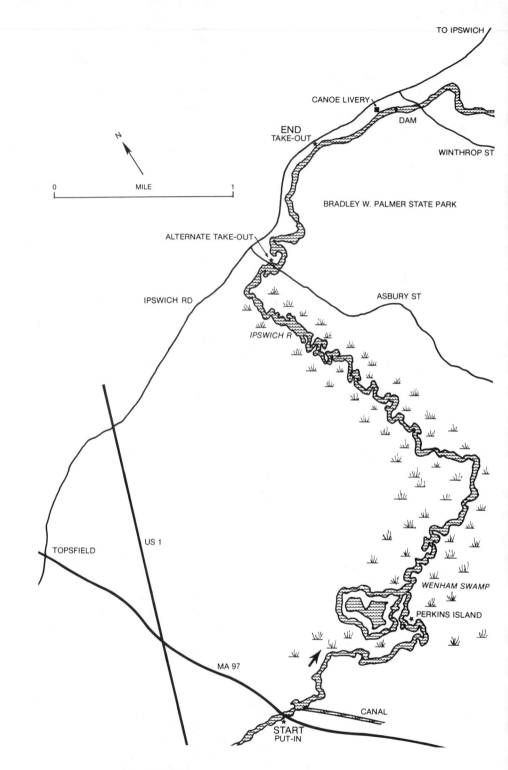

TO IPSWICH

CANOE LIVERY

DAM

WINTHROP ST

END
TAKE-OUT

BRADLEY W. PALMER STATE PARK

N

0   MILE   1

ALTERNATE TAKE-OUT

ASBURY ST

IPSWICH RD

IPSWICH R

WENHAM SWAMP

PERKINS ISLAND

TOPSFIELD

US 1

MA 97

CANAL

START
PUT-IN

50 *Massachusetts*

Make this trip in summer or early autumn, and you'll be accompanied by herons, bitterns, and sandpipers, the long-legged, long-billed birds that haunt such places. The entire swamp is a wildlife sanctuary and therefore protected.

Access

In summertime, the current of the river is usually so slow you can canoe upriver if you wish. Many people who use this river do just that, renting canoes from a livery on Ipswich Road, going upriver into the swamp and floating back down. You can do the same thing by driving along Ipswich Road just east of the village of Topsfield and putting in from one of the several access spots above the dam where the river runs parallel to the road. For a one-way trip, however, leave a car here or beside the bridge on nearby Asbury Street and then head west in another car to US 1. Turn left (south) on US 1 and follow it to MA 97. A left turn here and a short drive bring you to the river. A wide shoulder on the right just beyond the bridge is a good place to park, and a well-worn path provides easy access to the water.

The River

In low water it might be a bit scratchy going under the bridge, but you should stay afloat if you paddle down the middle of the river. Very quickly you'll pass beneath a railroad bridge and then see a wide and straight canal angling off to the right. As tempting as the canal might be, it won't take you to your car. Instead, take the shallow left fork, the regular river channel. In this early stretch, the canal may seem even more attractive because there are some snags and blowdowns in the river, but in a matter of minutes you'll be in deeper water and moving smoothly.

The river remains narrow as it winds its way between rocks and sandbars, flanked by willows and silver maples. Within half an hour of your start you will swing around a bend and pass a pine-crowned ridge on the right with a sign that identifies it as Perkins Island. Camping is permitted here only by reservation made through the Massachusetts Audubon Society. However, you may land and walk about. This is one of many such resting spots along the river. For the next mile or so, you'll have very pleasant paddling between forested shores. Oaks compete with maples for attention, and grape vines swarm over the lower bushes. You may see groups of people with binoculars along the left shore. Footpaths in this area are used extensively by bird-watchers checking out a marsh hidden from canoeists.

When you leave the woods behind and move out into the more open parts of the swamp, the river meanders back and forth in a series of hairpin turns. During the summer months, tall marsh plants will crowd the shoreline and limit your horizons. Colorful wildflowers, however, produce more than adequate compensation. Lavender loosestrifes of early autumn are particularly enchanting. These "weedy" areas are the favorite feeding grounds of the gangling, four-foot-tall great blue herons. Often you can follow one for a considerable distance down the river as it flees just one curve at a time ahead of your canoe.

Occasionally, short-cut channels will enable you to lop off some of the half circles, and from time to time you will return to woods briefly before breaking out into the open again. There are only a few homes visible from the river. When you pass an impressive estate high on a hill on the right, however, you'll be with in ½ mile or so of the Asbury Street bridge. You will also pass under a private wooden bridge belonging to the estate.

Asbury Street bridge About 20 or 30 minutes more of paddling around sharp turns brings you to Asbury Street. The bridge here is known locally as Palmer Bridge, for it is nearly at the front gate of Bradley W. Palmer State Park (no camping), which reaches down to the right shore of the river just beyond the bridge. If you are ending your trip here, the best take-out is on the left side just beyond the bridge.

Ipswich Road/end If you are continuing along the last leg toward the canoe livery or the Ipswich Road take-outs, just keep paddling. This final short stretch is possibly the most attractive of all, with majestic trees on both sides of the river. In fact, even if you left your car at Asbury Street, this segment is so pretty it is worth canoeing down toward the dam and back just to enjoy the surroundings.

7

Charles River
Medfield to South Natick

Put-In Point	Take-Out Point	Approximate Distance	Approximate Trip Time	Condition of Water	Portages
MA 109 bridge	Pleasant Street Picnic Area	10 miles	4 hours	Smooth	None

No canoeing guide for southern New England would be complete without a trip on the famed Charles River. The Charles has been a major transportation waterway since the founding of Boston, and in earlier centuries was the Indians' connecting link between the sea and inland Massachusetts. Yet, for all its popularity as a "city river" in Boston, it passes through long stretches of peaceful country. And just a few miles upriver from where sailboats and racing sculls crowd each other, you can enjoy tranquil day trips paddling through lush green lowlands and woodlands.

The Charles winds some 85 miles on its way to Boston Harbor. Most of it is canoeable, at least in spring, but the most attractive stretch is probably the 10-mile run from the MA 109 bridge at Medfield to the dam at South Natick. This is a trip well within the limits of novices and family groups, for there are no rapids or portages, and the current is smooth and moderate. Along the way, you will travel through marshy meadows, pass towering rock ledges, and float between shorelines decorated with imposing stands of maples, hemlocks, birches, and oaks. This trip of approximately 4 hours features man-made attractions as well as natural delights. You will paddle under old wooden bridges and trestles, pass the intriguing Death Bridge, then a statue perched on a ledge overlooking the river, and finally an elaborate footbridge before reaching your destination in South Natick.

Access

To leave a car at the take-out, drive on MA 16 into South Natick. At Pleasant Street, turn east, crossing the river just above the dam. Your take-out will be through a small picnic area on the river's shore. There is parking space for several cars along the street. After

The upper Charles is well within the limits of novices and family groups—and isn't bad for fishing either.

leaving a car, you can reach the recommended launching site by driving MA 16 southwest to MA 27, turning left, and following MA 27 into Medfield. There, turn right onto MA 109 and drive a short distance, until you cross the river. The best put-in is from the rear of a parking lot for a tavern called, appropriately enough, the Charles.

The River

Start/MA 109 bridge

From your launch site, the river flows for more than 2 miles through open marsh meadows, snaking its way back and forth through a generally treeless plain. Painted turtles and bullfrogs, soaking up the sunshine, are abundant along the shores here, and red-winged blackbirds that live in the tall marsh grasses keep up a spirited and raucous protest, particularly during nesting time.

About 20 minutes from the start you will encounter a break in the marshy terrain when you float under a bridge near Medfield Junction. Almost immediately, you will come to a railroad crossing set on wooden pilings. So much silt and debris has collected around the pilings over the years that most of the openings are now closed and you will have to go to the extreme left to find a suitable channel.

After passing through a small wooded area, you will return to the marshland. The river resumes meandering from the railroad bridge to the next landmark, the ominous-sounding Death Bridge. Earlier, when you drove MA 27 to the take-out in South Natick, you crossed this bridge, a modern structure that replaced an earlier bridge. A sign with the Death Bridge name formerly was displayed for passing motorists but is no longer in place. Legends have sprung up around the name, most of them dealing with grisly murders or tragic suicides. But the origin is far less dramatic. The bridge was named for a family—the Death family—that once lived nearby. The family eventually tired of problems with its name and changed it to Derth. The old name remains on the bridge, however—with or without the sign—adding a sense of foreboding to those who paddle beneath it.

Just minutes beyond Death Bridge you will find another railroad trestle, this one of rusty steel. Then, a few minutes later, you will arrive at one of the highlights of the trip, a rocky bluff on the left shore. The opportunity to take a break here and climb the bluff is almost irresistible, especially on sizzling summer days when the open marsh meadows can become virtual frying pans. (It is possible to put in at Death Bridge and skip the first few miles of this trip, but launching and parking are much more convenient at the MA 109 bridge.) There are a few scraggly trees clinging to the ledges—enough for some shade. Most canoeists tote their picnic fixings with them when they climb the bluff. It's the best spot on the trip for a leisurely rest.

Beyond the bluff the river makes a sweeping turn, almost a half-circle, around to the left. It then carries you through perhaps

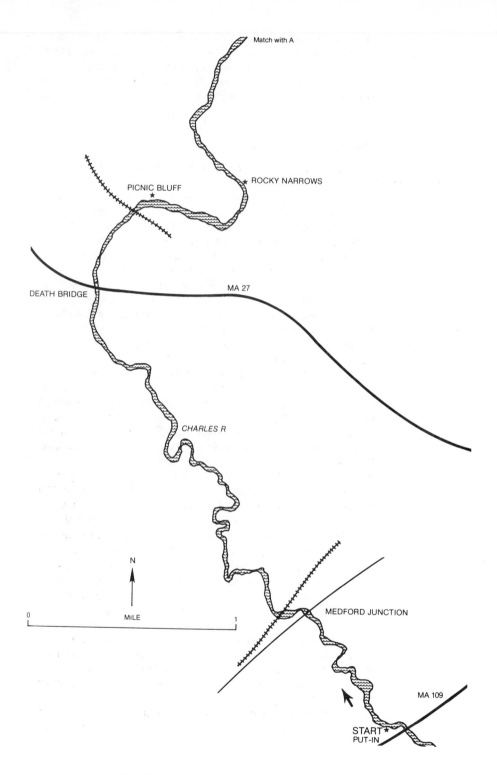

Match with A

ROCKY NARROWS

PICNIC BLUFF

DEATH BRIDGE

MA 27

CHARLES R

N

0   MILE   1

MEDFORD JUNCTION

MA 109

START
PUT-IN

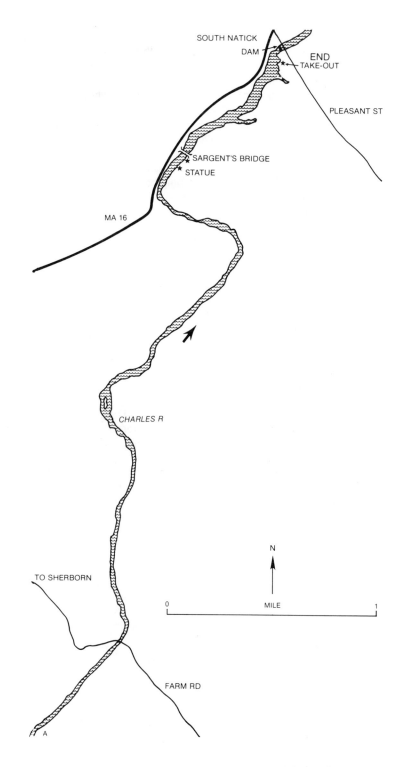

SOUTH NATICK
DAM
END
TAKE-OUT

PLEASANT ST

SARGENT'S BRIDGE
STATUE

MA 16

CHARLES R

N

TO SHERBORN

MILE

0   1

FARM RD

A

57 *Massachusetts*

the best-known area of this stretch, the Rocky Narrows. Here wooded bluffs crowd the river on both sides, although the water is still smooth and not particularly narrow. The bluff on the right at this point is frequently used as a picnic spot, but the attractiveness of its tall hemlocks is almost negated by sprawling vines of poison ivy.

You will continue to pass through delightful woodlands punctuated with glimpses of a few stately homes in the distance on the left. Then, about 20 minutes after paddling through Rocky Narrows, you will come to a low, picturesque bridge at Farm Road in Sherborn. This bridge not only has log pilings but also plank guardrails. Farm Road roughly follows the route of a famous Indian trail, the Connecticut Path. Beyond the bridge, you will pass a string of relatively new homes on the right. Fortunately, they do little to detract from the scenic value of the river. The water here is very shallow, with a rocky bottom, but paddling through remains easy in all but the driest of seasons.

As you near South Natick, there are more houses and a road (MA 16) on the left, but what catches your eye is the statue on the right. Standing just a few feet above the river on a boulder, the figure of a young woman in prayerful pose watches over the water. Just beyond is the elaborate, double-arched wooden footbridge known locally as Sargent's Bridge. Myths surround this area, too. Some townspeople say the statue commemorates a child who drowned near here. According to a South Natick historian, however, both the statue and the bridge were erected by Daniel Sargent, who owned a huge estate on the left side of the river and a farm on the right side. Wanting to preserve the beauty of the shoreline, he planted rhododendrons and other flowering trees, then added the statue as a finishing touch.

Pleasant Street Picnic Area/ end

After floating by several more elegant homes on the left, you will reach the deadwater from the dam. Paddle to the right side of the dam to your take-out at the small picnic area.

North River

Hanover to Norwell

Put-in Point	Take-out Points	Approximate Distance	Approximate Trip Time	Condition of Water	Portages
Riverside Drive	Chittenden Lane	7½ miles	2½-3 hours	Smooth (tidal)	None
Riverside Drive	Bridge Street	8 miles	3 hours	Smooth (tidal)	None
Riverside Drive	King's Landing	9 miles	3-3½ miles	Smooth (tidal)	None

The word "scenic" can be applied legitimately to many rivers in Massachusetts, including most of those found in this book, but for the North River, the term is not only proper but official. The North, a tidal river a short distance south of Boston, has recently been chosen for protection under Massachusetts's Scenic Rivers Act. The North is among the first waterways to be so designated by the Commonwealth. It deserves the honor.

The North River, which derives its name from a sister waterway called the South River that it joins where they together empty into the sea, is rich in history as well as physical attractions. Numerous shipyards crowded its banks from the late seventeenth century until after the Civil War. And for hundreds of years before that, Indian tribes used the North as a primary passage from the sea to inland Massachusetts and beyond. Most of the shipyards are gone now, and fiberglass and aluminum canoes have replaced the birchbark craft of the Indians, but the inexorable tides still surge in and out each day, making the North River a pleasant and interesting canoeing experience.

Access

Those planning to travel on the North have several options regarding trip distances. For one, the tides make this one of the easiest rivers on which to float both ways (be sure to check tide charts before starting out). Also, take-out points have been improved greatly in recent years. The last bridge before the river reaches the sea is MA 3A, but at that point the North is very wide and often crowded with powerboats. You can land at a marina by the MA 3A bridge, but

Wild iris hug the bank just beyond Hanover.

there is a fee for the privilege. The next bridge upriver, on Bridge Street, has two good take-outs but remember that the one on the north side of the river is for Norwell residents only. There is a good public launch on the southern side built recently by a Marshfield conservation organization. You can leave a car here for a trip of about 8 miles and 3 hours.

For a slightly longer journey, and a chance to see some of the best scenery along the river, look for a place called King's Landing at the end of a long gravel road running off MA 23, about $4/_{10}$ mile east of Bridge Street, in Norwell. There are canoes available for rent at King's Landing, making it easy to launch there, go upriver and return without hauling any gear at all.

If a shorter, one-way trip sounds good, you can take out at Chittenden Lane, about $1 1/_2$ miles upriver from King's Landing. This town-owned site with a wooden dock lies at the end of a narrow street, both sides of which are private property, so parking space is limited to a car or two. Both the Bridge Street and King's Landing sites are better.

Whether using King's Landing or Bridge Street as your take-out, you can reach the put-in in Hanover by driving MA 123 west until a fork just west of Bridge Street. Take the left fork, Dover Street, which soon ends at River Street. Follow River Street southwest (quickly passing Chittenden Lane) until you cross MA 53–MA 139 in Hanover, where River Street becomes Broadway. In just a short distance, Elm Street branches to the left off Broadway. Follow Elm Street until you reach the second of two side streets that carry the name Riverside Drive. Go left on Riverside to a large parking area along the riverbank. Many canoeists continue on Elm Street a bit farther, cross a bridge and put in below a dam, but if you use the Riverside Drive spot you will skip a stretch of narrow and shallow river that sometimes presents problems with rocks and blowdowns.

The River

Start/
Riverside
Drive

From the Riverside Drive put-in, the North almost immediately widens into the meandering marshland river that typifies its remaining miles. Low bushes and tall aquatic plants line both shores. Many of the plants add color during their blossoming periods, the blue and yellow wild irises being particularly eye catching. Tall trees form the background. Swallows and other birds add to the enchanting setting.

After about 30 minutes of paddling, you'll pass a canopied shoreside restaurant on the left and then several elegant homes before reaching the MA 53-MA 139 bridge. Here you will begin feeling the effects of the tide. If your timing is right—so you catch the tide as it retreats down the river—you will have an easy float. If the tide is still coming in, however, you will have to work.

Moments after passing the first bridge, you will paddle under a

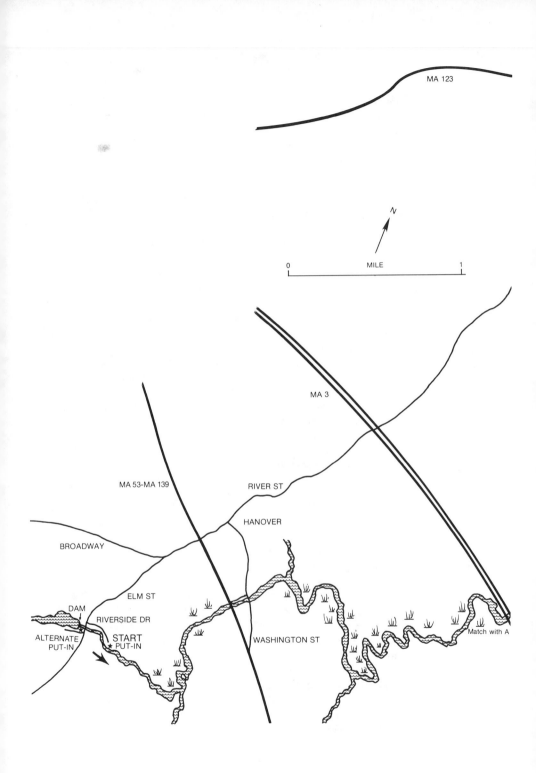

MA 123

N

0   MILE   1

MA 3

MA 53-MA 139

RIVER ST

HANOVER

BROADWAY

ELM ST

DAM

RIVERSIDE DR

ALTERNATE
PUT-IN

START
PUT-IN

WASHINGTON ST

Match with A

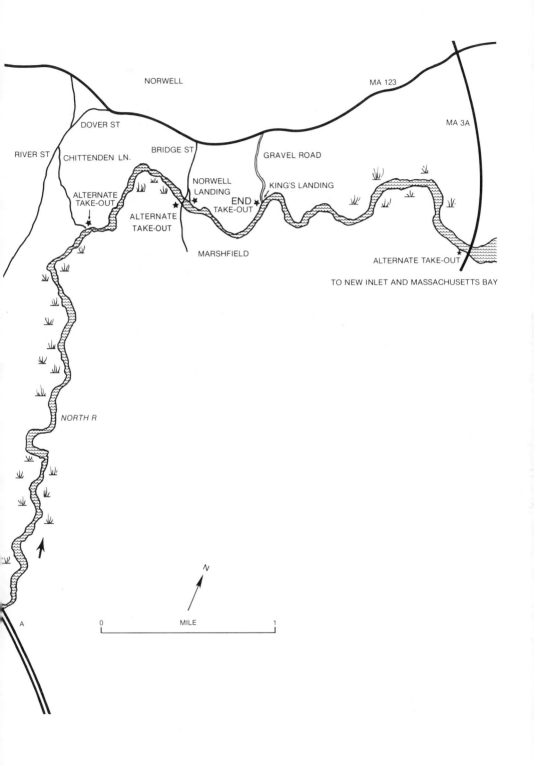

NORWELL

MA 123

DOVER ST

MA 3A

RIVER ST

CHITTENDEN LN.

BRIDGE ST

GRAVEL ROAD

NORWELL
LANDING

KING'S LANDING

ALTERNATE
TAKE-OUT

END
TAKE-OUT

ALTERNATE
TAKE-OUT

MARSHFIELD

ALTERNATE TAKE-OUT

TO NEW INLET AND MASSACHUSETTS BAY

NORTH R

N

0   MILE   1

A

63 *Massachusetts*

stone bridge at Washington Street, and then return to the open marshes. The river wanders back and forth over the 3 miles from Washington Street to the next set of bridges, the double span for MA 3. In this stretch during the summer you may see powerboats, some towing skiers. It is best to stay near the shore to avoid the boats speeding around blind bends, although the river is wide enough for both boats and canoes. The first of many signs along the left bank identifying sites of vanished shipyards are in this area also.

Beyond MA 3, the river, while still wide and open, becomes more interesting with several curves that take you near wooden knolls and hillsides on the right. These make fine picnic sites. Eventually, the river swings nearer trees and houses on the left, and you will pass more shipyard site signs. If you are taking out at Chittenden Lane, begin looking for the wooden dock on the left.

Chittenden Lane

If taking out at Bridge Street, head for the right shore as you paddle through the widening expanse near the bridge. The take-out is in a grove of trees just before you reach the bridge.

If going on to King's Landing, extra care is necessary when passing beneath the Bridge Street bridge for two reasons—the strong current under the bridge and the usual flurry of activity at the Norwell town landing just beyond the bridge on the left. The final leg of your trip to King's Landing is through an extremely attractive stretch that features a marshland on the left shore and a forest on the right. It may be this section, perhaps more than any other, that qualifies the North as an official scenic river.

King's Landing/ end

Taunton River

North Middleborough to Taunton

Put-in Point	Take-Out Point	Approximate Distance	Approximate Trip Time	Condition of Water	Portages
Titicut Street bridge	Raynham Crossing Plaza	12½ miles	4½-5 hours	Smooth, few riffles	None

If you like your canoeing on the leisurely side, with time to look around and plenty to look at, give the Taunton River in southeastern Massachusetts a try. The 12½-mile trip described here is one of the easiest in this book, and it offers a fascinating succession of natural attractions, particularly trees. On this stretch of the Taunton, from east of North Middleborough to the city of Taunton, you float through impressive old forests. These stands are intriguing both for their great variety of trees and for individual specimens, several of which are towering monarchs that must be from one to two hundred years old.

The river is recommended for beginners and family groups. The current is moderate, there are no portages, and there are no major rapids—although occasional stints of rock dodging will keep you alert. Even with frequent brief stops to examine the trees and a longer lunch break, this stretch is easily canoed in 4½ to 5 hours.

Access

Your take-out will be behind Raynham Crossing Plaza on US 44 at the eastern edge of Taunton. A driveway around the west side of the plaza leads to a suitable grassy spot at the river's edge. To haul your canoe to put-in, follow US 44 east to MA 18–MA 28, turn left (north) and drive 2 miles to Plymouth Street, which you then take right (east) a short distance to Titicut Street. Follow Titicut Street left (north) until it reaches the river. Best put-in is on the near side of the river, to the right of the road. However, if you wish to avoid the riffles under the bridge, you can put in over a guard rail on the left. If you are leaving a car at this end of the trip, there is room for parking several hundred feet beyond the bridge, on the right.

The River

At the put-in, you may face an obstacle right away. A string of rocks directly under the Titicut Street bridge forms a riffle. In high water, you can run it in the center, but when the water is down you may have to pull over to the left and line your canoe a few yards while walking on rocks at the foot of the abutment. Launching from the west side of the bridge avoids this riffle, but running it can be fun, and lining is easy. In any case, going under the bridge beats parking a car on the street or carrying the canoe up the steep bank and over the bridge.

The river is broad, smooth, and lined on both sides by thick woods, a condition that continues throughout most of the trip. There are no houses or cottages on the banks, just one old mill downriver at East Taunton, and no businesses are visible from the water until the final mile, when the river runs alongside US 44 into Taunton.

In summer, much of the distance between Titicut Street and the MA 18-MA 28 bridge is decorated with the showy purple spikes of pickerelweed, a plant that thrives at the shoreline. Look closely in

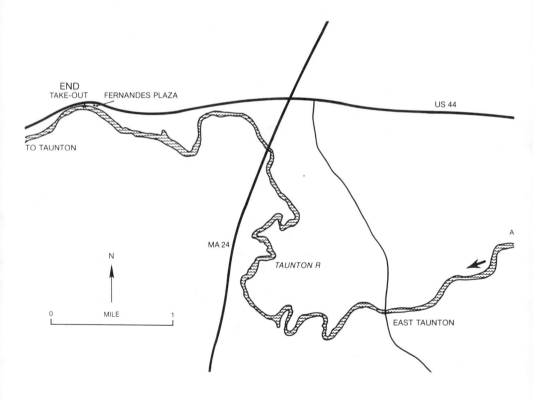

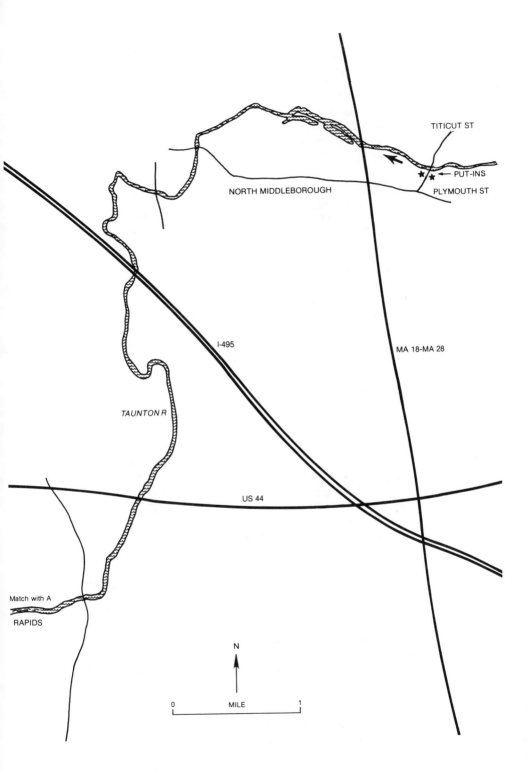

TITICUT ST

PUT-INS

PLYMOUTH ST

NORTH MIDDLEBOROUGH

I-495

MA 18-MA 28

TAUNTON R

US 44

Match with A

RAPIDS

N

0   MILE   1

67   *Massachusetts*

the shallow water at the base of the flower stalks; you are likely to see numerous big bullfrogs drowsily soaking up the sunshine, usually with just their heads above water. Make this trip on a summer evening, and you won't have to look for the frogs. You'll hear their bellowing chant long before you reach them.

Wildlife is quite abundant along the Taunton, even though the river runs through a heavily populated part of the state. On one midsummer cruise over these 12½ miles, we saw a mink, a great horned owl, several red-tailed hawks. a pair of mallard ducks, a wide assortment of songbirds, a sparrow hawk, several noisy kingfishers, and a mother wood duck that stashed its two half-grown youngsters in the weeds and then flopped along in front of our canoe for a quarter of a mile trying to lead us astray. In addition, raccoon tracks dotted the banks, and the shells of freshwater mussels, the object of the coons' forays, were easy to find. You can also see many muskrat tunnels in the banks when the water level is down.

But you are far more certain of seeing the big trees. These are close enough to the water so that you can pull over for a close look at almost any time. Many maples reach out over the river, their brilliant foliage making the Taunton an excellent autumn trip. Half a dozen species of oaks are here, too, including several gigantic swamp white oaks. There are groves of beeches, birches, pines, and hemlocks, and a great many hickory and walnut trees. The free nuts are another bonus on fall trips. Fall is the time for seeing the relatively rare tupelo or blackgum tree also, for then its leaves turn a fiery scarlet. The smooth floating gives you time to take a good look at all the trees.

Your first riffles after the Titicut Street bridge come about 2 miles from the start as you near a concrete bridge. These amount to very little, however; you can easily slip through at the center. Just beyond the bridge, on the left, is a string of majestic old maples, each one a giant. A break here is almost irresistible, even though it is still early in your trip.

You'll next come to a stretch of very shallow water punctuated with large boulders that are easy to maneuver past. Then you will pass beneath another bridge, float over more riffles, and in a few minutes reach the double bridges of I-495. This point is roughly 3½ miles from your start. The next several miles, during which you paddle under the US 44 bridge and on to East Taunton, are pleasant and easy, with one exception. While generally smooth water divides delightful forests with only an occasional patch of boulders to negotiate, perhaps the most difficult spot on the entire trip lies in this stretch, where a powerline crosses the river above the abutments of a vanished bridge. Here a short rapid interrupts the tranquility of the river. As soon as you spot the powerline you must make sure you swing to the right to run the rapid. In high water it can be run relatively smoothly, but in low water you may get hung up, or at least scrape bottom as you pass over the rocks.

At the East Taunton bridge you will reach back into history briefly as you pass a towering mill building. Note the extensive stonework laid up on the banks in the days when the river was harnessed by industry. The stonework, like the venerable old trees, invites closer inspection.

The river, prior to this point relatively straight, now takes a winding zigzag route to the MA 24 bridge, which is less than 3 miles from East Taunton. Here you will float into a few open areas and see some farms as well as wooded sections. Beyond the US 24 bridge you will have about 1½ miles of paddling in smooth water to your take-out spot on the right.

Raynham
Crossing
Plaza/end

10

Osterville Grand Island
Cotuit

Put-in and Take-out Point	Approximate Distance	Approximate Trip Time	Condition of Water	Portages
Old Shore Road	5½ miles	3 hours	Open bay, can be choppy	None

Canoeists not ready to put their paddles away when midsummer reduces inland rivers to shallow brooks would do well to head for Cape Cod. Numerous day trips are possible on the Cape's saltwater rivers, marshes, and inlets. All of these trips offer two strong attractions—refreshing relief from inland heat and delightful scenery. One of the better trips is a cruise around Osterville Grand Island, starting and ending at Cotuit. On this 5½-mile journey you paddle across three small bays and the length of a river while circling an island. You pass elegant mansions and float among hundreds of boats ranging from tiny skiffs to extravagant yachts. This trip is a unique experience, particularly for those accustomed to whitewater wilderness rivers.

Whitewater canoeists will immediately note two advantages to this trip. Instead of a wetsuit you can wear or bring along a swim suit, for there will be ample opportunities for cooling dips. And this trip can be completed without the car shuttling necessary on all quickwater river trips because you will begin and end at the same spot. Still, this is not a trip to undertake without careful planning. Because you will be paddling across open expanses, tides and winds are of primary importance. Check the marine forecast and forego the trip if winds are expected to be heavier than 10 or 15 knots. Similarly, plan your trip with an eye on the tides. Ideally, you should begin a few hours before high tide so that you will be riding an incoming tide as you cover the final stretch back to Cotuit. High tide times for Cotuit Bay are listed in local Cape newspapers, and major newspapers in southern New England show high tides for Hyannis Port, which is just a few miles to the east.

The Soprano of Osterville lies at dockside as the drawbridge to Grand Island opens to permit another sailboat passage to the sea.

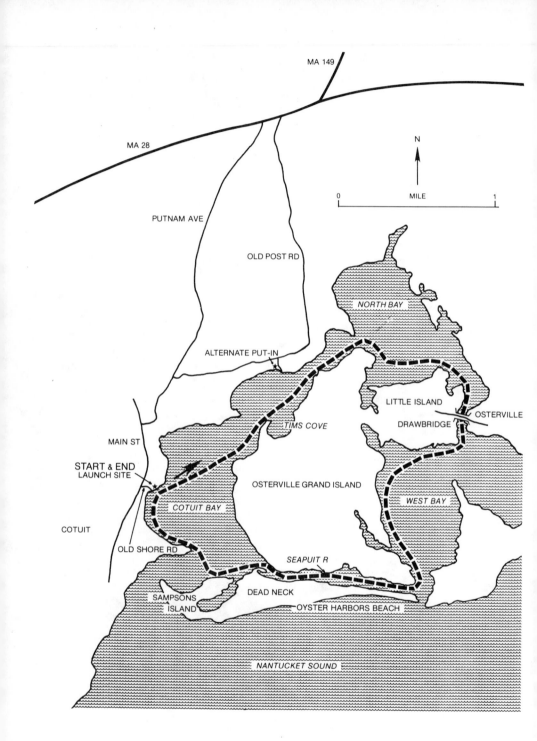

MA 149

MA 28

N

PUTNAM AVE

0   MILE   1

OLD POST RD

NORTH BAY

ALTERNATE PUT-IN

LITTLE ISLAND

OSTERVILLE

DRAWBRIDGE

TIMS COVE

MAIN ST

START & END
LAUNCH SITE

OSTERVILLE GRAND ISLAND

WEST BAY

COTUIT BAY

COTUIT

OLD SHORE RD

SEAPUIT R

SAMPSONS
ISLAND

DEAD NECK

OYSTER HARBORS BEACH

NANTUCKET SOUND

72   *Massachusetts*

Access

To reach your put-in point, take MA 149 (Exit 5) south off US 6 to MA 28, turn right, and drive a short distance to Putnam Avenue. Go left on Putnam Avenue until you reach Main Street, where you turn left. Drive to Old Shore Road, which leads to a public landing. There is also a public landing off Old Post Road, which also turns off MA 28 (see sketch map), but the Old Shore Road launch site is considerably larger and more interesting. If you arrive early in the day—which you should do because the wind normally picks up as the day progresses —you will find a fleet of boats moored near the landing. There are usually dozens of small sailboats and powerboats here, sleek and sporty craft, but a far cry from the luxurious boats you will see later.

The Trip

Start/
Old Shore
Road

You can paddle either way around the island, of course, but it is best to go left through Cotuit Bay and North Bay, then south through West Bay, west through the Seapuit River,and back north through the lower part of Cotuit Bay. By taking this route you have the advantage not only of the incoming tide as you near the finish, but also the prevailing south to southwest wind at your back at a time when you will appreciate such help the most. Unless you are fighting tides or wind more than necessary, this trip will take about 3 hours, including time for a lunch break (but not swimming breaks).

As you begin, look across the bay and set your sights on a sand cliff on the island. When you reach the base of the cliff, start following the shoreline and you will begin seeing the large homes perched above, most with winding stairways down to the water. There are many trees on the island and a surprising number of birds—egrets, sandpipers, killdeer, herons, red-winged blackbirds, even quail—but it will be the fine homes that hold your attention. The houses continue to appear at regular intervals as you paddle through the narrow neck of Cotuit Bay and enter North Bay. Here a sign in the water indicates a ski area; it is wise to stay close to shore here to absorb the wake of the ski tow boats. As you round a point you will see an inlet on the right, but do not take it—it is a dead end. Instead, swing around Little Island, which is merely an extension of Grand Island, and get ready for heavy traffic.

At the east end of Little Island there are several marinas and a great many boats of all sizes and descriptions. If they were all underway at the same time, it's doubtful if you could maneuver a canoe through this area. That is seldom the case, however, and a float through here is a pleasant venture into a world of seagoing vessels. Larger boats move very slowly in this area; you are in no danger of being swamped or run over if you stay out of the main channel. Next is the drawbridge for the only road that connects the island with the mainland. Large powerboats and sailboats with tall masts signal to have the bridge raised with three blasts of their horns. No, the bridge isn't raised for canoes.

Beyond the drawbridge, you will enter West Bay, which is wide, shallow, and usually filled with sailboats. You will now be heading south , into the wind, so it is best to paddle close to the island shore on the right. This will provide protection from the breezes and also views of more impressive homes. When you pass a sandbar guarding a narrow inlet, just before a point, you will be nearing the Seapuit River and the mouth of West Bay, which empties into Nantucket Sound. Stay close to the right shore, and just after passing a huge home with tennis courts and a cabana at the water's edge, swing into the river.

There is some boat traffic in the narrow river, but speeds are limited to 6 miles an hour or less, so there is little wake. At this point, a part of the inviting Oyster Harbors Beach is on your left, separating the river from the sound. This is where canoeists often pull ashore for lunch or swimming. A short distance farther, you will see signs on the beach indicating a wildlife sanctuary on Sampson's Island; access here is prohibited without a special permit from the Massachusetts Audubon Society. The river is about a mile long, and throughout its length the island shore on the right features piers, elegant homes and clubs, and the kinds of boats most of us only wish we could afford.

As you leave the river, passing a sign in the water that says "Caution, Dogs Swimming," keep to the left along the beach shore, particularly if the bay is choppy. Continue following the beach until you are opposite a point extending from the mainland to the north. Then, with great care because you will be crossing a channel that carries much boating traffic, cross over to the point. Once you reach the point you will be protected from the wind, but you will still have heavy traffic to deal with on the final leg because your route takes you past the Cotuit town dock and the large number of boats that use it. An equal flurry of activity will greet you at the public landing, but by this time you'll be so accustomed to paddling through a maze of boats you will feel right at home.

Old Shore Road/end

Trips in
Rhode Island

11

Blackstone River
Albion to Lonsdale

Put-in Point	Take-Out Point	Approximate Distance	Approximate Trip Time	Condition of Water	Portages
Albion Dam	John St., Lonsdale	5 miles	2½ hours	Mostly smooth	Ashton Dam

Canoe trips on the Blackstone River in northern Rhode Island continue to get better and better. Once considered among America's most polluted rivers because of the mills and factories along its shores, the Blackstone now runs cleaner than at any time in a century.

In addition, recent development of the Blackstone River State Park in this area, particularly where the river is joined by the historic Blackstone Canal, make this a thoroughly pleasant ride. You can now get around one dam by going a short distance into the canal and using new stone steps, and if you wish, you can avoid another dam and a possible long carry by taking the canal a couple of miles.

The Blackstone River enters Rhode Island just north of Woonsocket and runs through Pawtucket and eventually into Narragansett Bay. In the early days, the river was the primary means of both transportation and power for the area. Unfortunately, the many mills it spawned during the textile boom of years ago nearly destroyed the river, and it took great efforts on the part of hundreds of volunteers, along with the closing of most of the old mills, to bring the river back to life.

Now, canoeing the broad river is enjoyable again. And it appears the improvements will be continuing. As the state park work progresses, more access points will be made and portages will be easier.

Because there is no longer a good put-in at Manville, I now suggest starting at Albion and running to Lonsdale. That is a distance of about 5 miles. To see more of the river and its resurgent wildlife, you can extend the trip on both ends: by going upriver from Albion to the Manville Dam, then returning, and at the end of your trip by floating into the Lonsdale Marsh before returning to the take-out.

If you do not go upriver from Albion, the only portage is an easy

The author putting in after the carry around Ashton Dam.

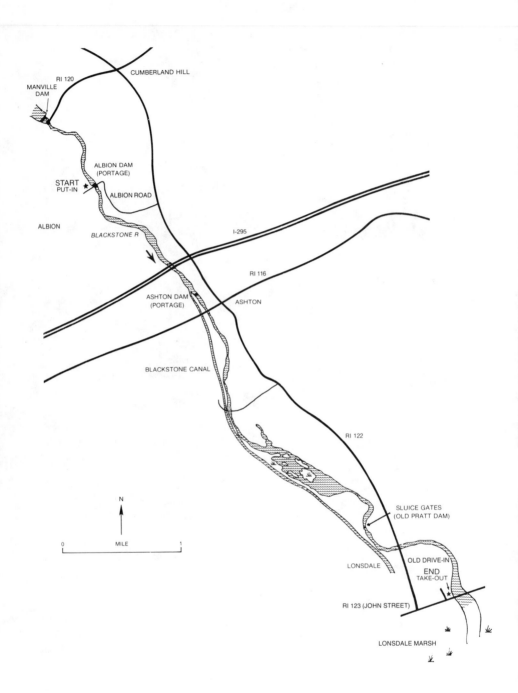

CUMBERLAND HILL

RI 120

MANVILLE
DAM

ALBION DAM
(PORTAGE)

START
PUT-IN

ALBION ROAD

ALBION

BLACKSTONE R

I-295

RI 116

ASHTON DAM
(PORTAGE)

ASHTON

BLACKSTONE CANAL

RI 122

N

0   MILE   1

SLUICE GATES
(OLD PRATT DAM)

OLD DRIVE-IN

LONSDALE

END
TAKE-OUT

RI 123 (JOHN STREET)

LONSDALE MARSH

one at Ashton. Inexperienced canoeists, however, may want to avoid the old Pratt Dam near Lonsdale as well. It has open sluice gates that some canoeists run, but doing so can be dangerous and spills are frequent.

The only fast water, other than at Pratt Dam, is just below the other dams and beneath the RI 116 and Martin Street bridges. These areas are usually mere riffles but occasionally increase up to Class II rapids.

Access

Your take-out is in Lonsdale, below the bridge for RI 123 (John Street). Park at the entrance to the old Lonsdale Drive-in Theater. The carry down to the river is not particularly easy but it is the best currently available. State officials have been attempting to acquire a better take-out spot in the area but at present more suitable places are private property.

Start/
Albion
Dam

To reach the put-in, drive RI 123 west about a block to RI 122, which you then follow north about 4½ miles to Albion Road on the left. Follow Albion Road until it crosses the river. Just beyond the bridge is a gravel lane running to the right, toward the Albion Dam. The easiest spot to put in is just below the dam. However, in low water, this area might be too rocky and you may have to choose a place nearer the Albion Road bridge.

If planning to add a ride upriver toward Manville, put in just above the dam.

The River

Before starting downriver, you might want to go upriver for awhile. The 1½-mile stretch between Albion and Manville is flatwater and wooded shores. We canoe it sometimes just for the wildlife— herons and sandpipers stalk the shallows, kingfishers rattle across the river and orioles and thrushes sing from the shoreline trees. There also are big snapping turtles in this section along with a great many bullfrogs.

Below Albion Dam, you pass under Albion Road and then under a railroad bridge. A huge brick building on the right, origi- nally a mill but now a housing complex, is about all you can see of the village of Albion from the water.

For most of the run to the next dam, you paddle between attrac- tive shores accented with large trees, vibrant mountain laurel thickets, and rock outcroppings. The water is smooth and easy.

Ashton
Dam

After passing under the high bridge for I-295, you are nearing the Ashton Dam. Look for stonework and guardrails on the right— they mark the entrance to the Blackstone Canal. It is just before the dam and before you reach the towering, arching viaduct for RI 116.

Since the development of the Blackstone River State Park, it's an easy matter to float into the canal. At the point where the stone retaining wall ends on the left, there are steps to enable canoeists to carry their boats back to the river.

It's important at this point to decide whether you want to try running the sluice gates at Pratt Dam, still two miles ahead. If you'd rather play it safe, stay in the canal, which was built in the 1820s. In all but extremely high water, the canal provides an easy paddle all the way to Lonsdale. In high water, you may have to portage around the Martin Street bridge. Farther ahead, you will have to carry over a low road built across the canal long after it was abandoned to boat traffic.

The canal eventually runs beneath buildings in Lonsdale. Follow it as far as you can, then take out on the left and return to the river. It's not a particularly easy portage but might be preferable to running the old Pratt Dam, which you can see as soon as you climb the canal bank.

For those who choose the river route from the Ashton Dam, you'll have a longer route because the river makes two sweeping curves to the left. There are "boney" areas beneath both the RI 116 and Martin Street bridges—in both cases, stay near the right shore—and you'll have to pick your way through a couple of other "rock gardens." For the most part, though, it's a fairly easy paddle until reaching Pratt Dam.

You reach the dam just as the river makes a sharp turn left. There are five sluice gates and the river roars through them with whitewater fury. All canoeists should pull out on the right and walk ahead to check the openings very carefully for branches or other debris that might be caught in the passages. More than one canoeists has been dumped by such obstacles and a dumping here, with the water crashing through the narrow gates, can be dangerous.

Unfortunately, carrying around the dam is difficult because of the high retaining walls on both sides of the river. Whether you choose the right bank or the left, you will have a carry of about 200 yards.

When the gates are clear, the run through can be exhilarating, even though you are likely to get doused by the backwash and standing waves just below the dam.

In a few more minutes, you will pass under the RI 122 bridge and begin making the horseshoe curve around what was the Lonsdale Drive-in Theater. Two movie screens can still be seen through the trees on the right.

The next bridge is for RI 123 (John Street) and is your take-out point, but you may want to continue into Lonsdale Marsh, one of the "wildest" wetlands in this part of the state. The many coves are home to ducks, geese, swans, egrets, herons, bitterns, marsh wrens, red-winged blackbirds, and assorted other birds. With the smooth water, a return to your take-out is easy.

Lonsdale/
end

Pettaquamscutt (Narrow) River

Narragansett

Put-In Point	Take-Out Points	Approximate Distance	Approximate Trip Time	Condition of Water	Portages
Gilbert Stuart Landing	Middle Bridge	5 miles	2 hours	Smooth (tidal)	None
Gilbert Stuart Landing	Cement Bridge	5¾ miles	2½ hours	Smooth (tidal)	None

In canoeing the Pettaquamscutt, or Narrow River, as it is known to most Rhode Islanders, you will travel through a 200-year span in less than 3 hours. Your start will be beside an eighteenth-century landmark that features clapboard-covered buildings and a grinding waterwheel, and you can end the trip riding the ocean surf in the company of sleek, modern powerboats.

The Pettaquamscutt, only about 6 miles long, runs parallel to Narragansett Bay entirely within the town of Narragansett. This area is just above southeastern Rhode Island's most popular beaches and the fishing villages of Point Judith and Galilee. The Pettaquamscutt is a tidal river, so you should check a tide chart before attempting this trip. Canoeing 6 miles against the tide can be hard work, but floating with it makes this trip one of the easier ones in Rhode Island. To catch the outgoing current, start shortly after high tide, which is about 5 minutes earlier in Narragansett than at Newport. Tidal data for Newport is given in local newspapers.

Access

You have a choice of take-outs. You can drive US 1 to Middle Bridge Road, turn east and drive for 2 miles, and then park beside Middle Bridge (this is the second of three bridges over the Pettaquamscutt, hence the name). Or you can continue across Middle Bridge, turn right on US 1A, and leave a car beside the next bridge, which is officially named Governor Sprague Bridge but usually referred to locally as Cement Bridge. River access from the highway is good just before and just after the bridge, both on the right side. The extra stretch of river between Middle Bridge and Cement Bridge adds only $3/_4$ mile of canoeing, but makes it much easier to explore a large cove between the two bridges. Also, Cement Bridge serves as a more convenient take-out if you wish to paddle on out to the ocean, which is less than a mile away.

To reach put-in, return to US 1 and drive north to Gilbert Stuart Road (just south of RI 138) and turn east. Immediately after Gilbert Stuart Road crosses a small stream at the bottom of a steep hill, look on the right for a sign indicating Gilbert Stuart Landing. This landing will be your parking lot and launch site. Stuart names dominate the area because Gilbert Stuart, one of America's foremost portrait painters of the post-Revolution era, was born in the farmhouse just across the road from the landing. It is worth taking time to visit the restored home and mills of Stuart's youth either before or after your canoe trip. A guided tour of the buildings and grounds is available for a small fee. In addition to the house, with its eighteenth-century furnishings and numerous reproductions of Stuart's most famous paintings, you will also get a look at a grist mill, an Indian burial ground, and a waterwheel that still turns, keeping the snuff mill on the ground floor of the house operable. This snuff mill, the first in New England, was constructed by Stuart's father shortly after he arrived in 1751. Gilbert Stuart was born in 1755 and lived here until he was thirteen years old.

The River

Start/
Gilbert
Stuart
Landing

At your start, the Pettaquamscutt (an Indian word meaning "big, round rock" and referring to a huge granite ledge just west of here, but not visible from the water) is not only narrow but also very shallow. Gilbert Stuart Brook joins another stream here in forming the river. You may have to line your canoe a short distance before hopping in. Quickly, though, you will emerge onto a large pond and you'll be on your way. The water is generally clear here and the paddling is easy. At this point, you will not be affected much by the tides.

Paddle toward the narrow gap on the south side of the pond. Once through this gap, which is shallow but canoeable even at low tide, you will begin to feel the effects of the tide. You will be in another pondlike expanse that may make you wonder why anybody would nickname the Pettaquamscutt the Narrow River. This section is perhaps the prettiest of the trip, with wooded shores on both sides. There are several houses along the left bank, but the right side is almost parklike with stately trees parading down a long slope to the water. If you are floating the outgoing tide, and are not confronted with the strong headwinds that sometimes sweep upriver, you will reach a bridge in slightly more than an hour from your start. This is the Bridgetown Road bridge.

You may have to dodge fishing poles and lines as you make your way beneath the Cement Bridge.

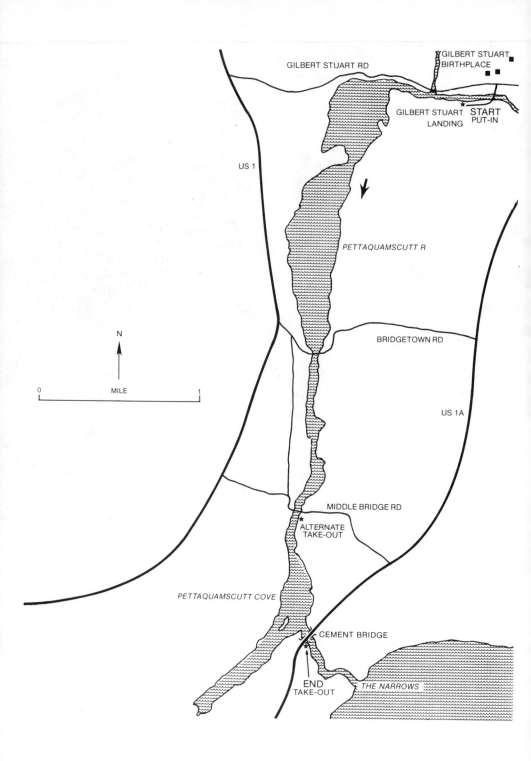

GILBERT STUART RD

GILBERT STUART
BIRTHPLACE

GILBERT STUART
LANDING

START
PUT-IN

US 1

PETTAQUAMSCUTT R

N

0   MILE   1

BRIDGETOWN RD

US 1A

MIDDLE BRIDGE RD

ALTERNATE
TAKE-OUT

PETTAQUAMSCUTT COVE

CEMENT BRIDGE

END
TAKE-OUT

THE NARROWS

Beyond this first bridge, the river narrows considerably and is flanked on both sides by houses, many of which feature docks and a boat or two. On summer weekends, you may find the boating traffic in this area too heavy for pleasant canoeing. One building on the left is worth looking for, a small green shed about ¼ mile beyond the bridge. Installed in its wall is a clock with a face about four feet across. This old tower clock was rescued by the man who owns the property, a retired watchsmith who says he built the shed for the clock and keeps it running for his own enjoyment. But boaters and canoeists using the river benefit from the clock, too. Far fewer now are late getting home for supper.

You will continue to see houses along the right shore for the remaining 2 miles to Middle Bridge. The left shore, however, soon opens into an area dotted with tiny estuaries. Many of these can be explored by canoe at high tide. When the tide is out, the exposed mud flats attract numerous egrets, herons, sandpipers, and other shorebirds.

Middle Bridge   If the water is low as you near Middle Bridge, keep to the left to remain in the main channel. The right side is quite shallow. Note, too, that you may have to dodge fishing lines as you pass under the bridge. This is one of the area's most popular fishing spots, particularly in early spring when the flatfish are hitting. Indeed, it is rare to see this bridge without at least one fisherman. Flounder and striped bass also are caught in the river, and its upper reaches near Gilbert Stuart's birthplace are famous locally for the annual run of buckies, or alewives.

You can take out on the left if Middle Bridge is your destination. If you are going on to Cement Bridge, however, follow the channel as it curves left for the final ¾ mile. First, though, you may want to spend some time exploring Pettaquamscutt Cove and its islands off to the right. The cove is shallow and bird life around the low islands is usually abundant, so a leisurely side trip can be most enjoyable.

Cement Bridge/ end   Once you reach Cement Bridge, you have another option. You can take out immediately just before the bridge, on either the left or the right, depending on where you parked, or you can follow the river all the way to the sea and then return. There are some rocks at the mouth, called The Narrows, and generally plenty of surf. Experienced canoeists often come here in summer for canoe-surfing— paddling out through the waves and riding them back in. In rough seas, though, this is a sport best left to the experts.

Great Swamp

South Kingstown

Put-in Point	Take-Out Points	Approximate Distance	Approximate Trip Time	Condition of Water	Portages
Taylor's Landing	Worden's Pond Road	5½ miles	2-2½ hours	Smooth, open pond	None
Taylor's Landing	Biscuit City Road	7 miles	4-4½ hours	Smooth, open pond	None

The Great Swamp, located in the southern part of Rhode Island, provides perhaps the most intriguing canoe trip in the state. The trip is an excursion into hidden junglelike retreats that cannot be reached any other way. Here, you will float into a vast state-owned management area on one river, paddle across a shallow but wide pond, and then finish your trip on another river that snakes its way through dense vine-draped vegetation. There will be no doubt in your mind why this area is called Great Swamp.

Two routes are available. The full 7-mile trip includes portions of the Chipuxet and Charles rivers and Worden's Pond. A shorter version of about 5½ miles takes the Chipuxet to Worden's Pond, and then follows the pond's southern shoreline to a landing. The shorter trip takes only about 2½ hours, but it misses the fascinating atmosphere of the winding Charles, as well as a lunch break on a picturesque point jutting out into the pond and a stopover at a wildlife marsh where ospreys, a relatively rare bird, can be spotted.

Access

The put-in for both trips is Taylor's Landing, a state launching area on RI 138 in West Kingston. If you are making the short trip, you reach the take-out by driving east on RI 138 from Taylor's Landing to RI 110, and then going south to Worden's Pond Road, which you follow west

Chipuxet River, which flows into Worden's Pond, at the beginning of the Great Swamp trip.

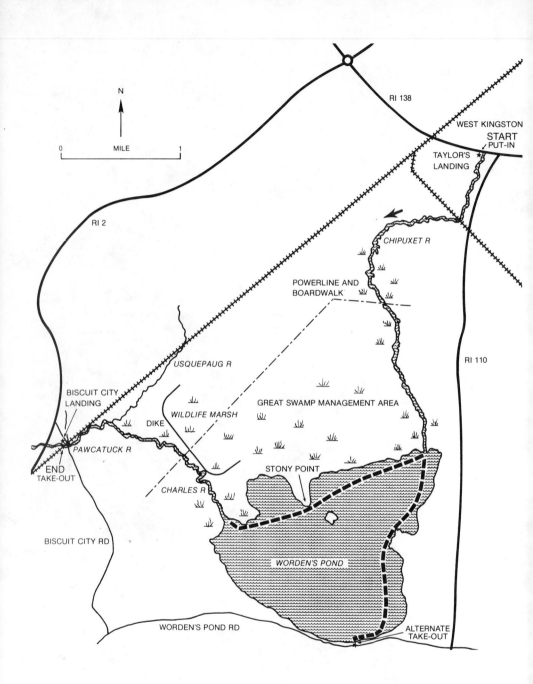

N

0   MILE   1

RI 138

WEST KINGSTON
START
PUT-IN

TAYLOR'S
LANDING

RI 2

CHIPUXET R

POWERLINE AND
BOARDWALK

RI 110

USQUEPAUG R

BISCUIT CITY
LANDING

GREAT SWAMP MANAGEMENT AREA

DIKE

WILDLIFE MARSH

PAWCATUCK R

END
TAKE-OUT

STONY POINT

CHARLES R

BISCUIT CITY RD

WORDEN'S POND

WORDEN'S POND RD

ALTERNATE
TAKE-OUT

to the landing at the pond's edge. If you are making the full 7-mile trip, drive west from Taylor's Landing to RI 2, turn south, and continue around the swamp to Biscuit City Road. A short drive on this secondary road will take you to a state landing beside a railroad track. There is plenty of room here for your car.

The River

Start/
Taylor's
Landing Back at Taylor's Landing, you launch on the Chipuxet, a stream that is so narrow for the first several hundred yards you must almost pull yourself through by grasping the shoreline bushes. There are similar areas ahead, too, so it is best to make this trip in spring before the heavy summer growth reduces the river's width. Water depth remains fairly constant throughout the warmer months, however, so you can canoe here during the summer if you don't mind wielding a machete occasionally. Less than ½ mile from its brushy beginning, the Chipuxet opens into a pleasant little river. The current will carry your canoe along, and all you have to do is steer around the numerous turns. There are no rapids here or anywhere else on this trip, no carries, and very few rocks to worry about. You occasionally come to logs and blowdowns, but they present few problems.

You will pass under an abandoned railroad bridge, and then make several sweeping turns before floating beneath an old wooden boardwalk that follows a power line through the swamp. Here taller trees edge the banks but they soon give way again to smaller bushes. Off to the sides are many shallow water pockets that are ideal for the wood ducks and mallards you are likely to flush in spring. Muskrats and raccoons also abound in this area, and if you are quiet—and very lucky—you might spot a deer coming down to the river for a drink.

When you reach Worden's Pond, slightly more than 3 miles from your put-in, you are in for a different type of canoeing. This 1,000-acre pond is very shallow, but paddling across it can be work, particularly if you are heading into the wind, which seems to be the case more often than not. If your take-out is Worden's Pond Road, follow the left shore around to the landing. If you are going on to Biscuit City Road, however, your immediate goal is Stony Point, a rock-ribbed finger of land slightly to the right of center as you face the pond. Stony Point points almost directly out toward the lone island in the pond. The point can be reached in a few minutes on a calm day, but on a windy day the journey may require a half hour or more of hard paddling.

Stony Point is a good place to stop, even if you don't need a rest. The large round boulders scattered about make natural picnic tables, and laurel growing along the shore offers flowers in June and greenery all year. From the point, you will also have a panoramic view of the pond and the privately owned island, which features a small red cabin.

To resume your trip, paddle to the right immediately upon leaving the point, and head for another, less-conspicuous point across a cove. This finger of land is just a short paddle away; when you round it you will see the mouth of the stream that you will take out of the pond. On some maps it is called the Pawcatuck River, but most local residents call this section the Charles River and save the Pawcatuck name for a larger river (see Trip 15) farther west that is formed by the confluence of this stream and a couple of other smaller ones.

By whatever name, this steam is a good practice course for backwatering and maneuvering around bends. It is nothing but turns, a succession of hairpins that can be a delight for the experienced canoeist, but a challenge (or headache) for the novice. The Charles is even narrower than the Chipuxet, and grape vines swing so low across the water you may have to duck occasionally to get through. Add the greenbrier vines that swarm over the shoreline bushes and you have a setting likely to conjur up images of monkeys, crocodiles and other tropical animals. But relax; the only "wild animals" that may be a problem are mosquitoes. Fortunately, hundreds of swallows and other birds do their best to take care of that situation.

When the river swings near a high earthen dike on the right, tie up and climb the bank. This dike surrounds an expansive marsh created by the state as a wildlife refuge. The marsh is the home of numerous waterfowl as well as ospreys, the big fish-eating hawks that balance their bulky nests on power-line poles above the water. You can walk either direction on the dike for some distance if you wish. It is part of a well-known hiking trail. However, do not put your canoe in the marsh; it is for the birds only.

As you resume your trip on the Charles, you will find the river becoming even more crooked. It is slightly wider than the stretch near the pond, though, making the maneuvering a bit easier. Shortly after passing another section of the power-line boardwalk, you will meet on the right another river that also has two names here: the Usquepaug and the Queens. Go left, with the current.

You will find the river wider the rest of the way, but there are still few straight stretches. When you see a railroad track on the right, you are nearing the take-out. Don't swing into the first channel to the right—it's a dead end. Paddle to the left instead. After a few more turns, you will return to the railroad line and soon you will see a tree standing in the shallow water with a sign "Boat Landing" and **Biscuit** an arrow pointing to the right. Leave the main channel for the inlet, **City** and then turn right into a narrow stream that runs under the rail- **Landing/** road tracks. Biscuit City Landing is on your left, just beyond the **end** railroad tracks.

Wood River

Exeter to Alton

Put-in Points	Take-out Points	Approximate Distance	Approximate Trip Time	Condition of Water	Portages
RI 165 bridge	Wyoming Dam	5½ miles	2½-3 hours	Mostly fast, some smooth	Barberville Dam
RI 165 bridge	Alton Dam	13½ miles	6-6½ hours	Fast, smooth, some open ponds	4 dams, one long carry
Hope Valley Road Landing	Alton Dam	6 miles	3 hours	Mostly smooth	Woodville Dam

Ask any Rhode Island outdoorsman for a good place to canoe in his state, and invariably the reply will begin, "Well, there's the Wood River..." The Wood deserves such recognition, for it has just about everything family canoeists look for. There is some quickwater and much smooth water, some open pond paddling and some maneuvering around logs and blowdowns, some shady forest stretches and several lush swamps, and even a number of little villages to visit along the route. Unfortunately, there also are several dams on the Wood River that must be carried around, but most of these portages are relatively easy and provide breaks from the paddling. You have a choice of several good put-in and take-out spots, so you can vary the distance of your trip easily.

The Wood runs through the southwestern part of Rhode Island, and eventually joins the Pawcatuck (see Trip 15) in flowing to the sea. Canoeing can begin as far north as the RI 165 bridge in Exeter and continue to Alton, which is just above the junction with the Pawcatuck. This trip is approximately 13½ miles long, takes about 6½ hours to paddle, and includes carries around four dams. Because of the difficult portages in the middle segment, however, many canoeists divide the trip into two, taking out at Wyoming, skipping a mile of river obstructed by dams and low water, and then launching again at Hope Valley.

Access

If you are planning to make the full-length trip, your take-out will be at a state landing on RI 91 just west of a dam in the village of Alton. You can reach your put-in point by following RI 91 east to Wood River Junction, going north on Hope Valley Road to RI 3 in the village of Hope Valley, then driving on RI 3 north to RI 165. A turn left (west) will take you to the river in a few miles. Access and parking are available on a gravel lane that runs along the east side of the river.

Canoeists who prefer avoiding the portages between Wyoming and Hope Valley can do so quite easily. For the take-out, leave a car at the state landing beside Wyoming Dam on RI 3 while doing the upper Wood; then retrieve your cars and shuttle them to the downriver points. Take-out would be beside the Alton Dam as mentioned above, and the put-in for the lower segment, which is approximately 6 miles long, would be from a gravel landing along Hope Valley Road, just south of the I-95 overpass.

The River

Start/
RI 165
bridge

Even in spring, the first stretch below RI 165 may require some lining as the river is very narrow and shallow. But soon you will find yourself on a quick little stream that winds through attractive woodlands. This is the state's best-known trout stream; you will undoubtedly meet fishermen here in April and May. The area is good bird habitat, too, and you are likely to see many migrating warblers and ducks, and perhaps hear grouse drumming in the woods. The forest opens into a marshy area at what is called Frying Pan Pond. Just beyond, you'll see houses on the shore and then a dam and bridge. This is the community of Barberville. Take out on the left. Accomplished canoeists can put in again immediately below the dam and float under the bridge, but the current is very strong here and there are enough rocks in the riverbed to make this stretch hazardous to beginners. The safest portage is to cross the bridge to a path that runs along the right side of the river.

Barberville
Dam

Once back on the water, you will soon pass through the rougher riffles, but the quickwater continues for some distance before the river widens again. Then after gliding under a very low bridge at Dyer Hill Road, you'll enter Wyoming Pond, a long reservoir backed up behind Wyoming Dam. Paddle along the left shore of the pond to the take-out point at the dam.

Wyoming
Dam

Putting in again just beyond the Wyoming Dam is virtually impossible because of shallow water and a long stretch of rocks. It is better to carry your gear a few hundred yards down RI 3 to the

The Wood is perhaps the most delightful river to canoe in all of Rhode Island.

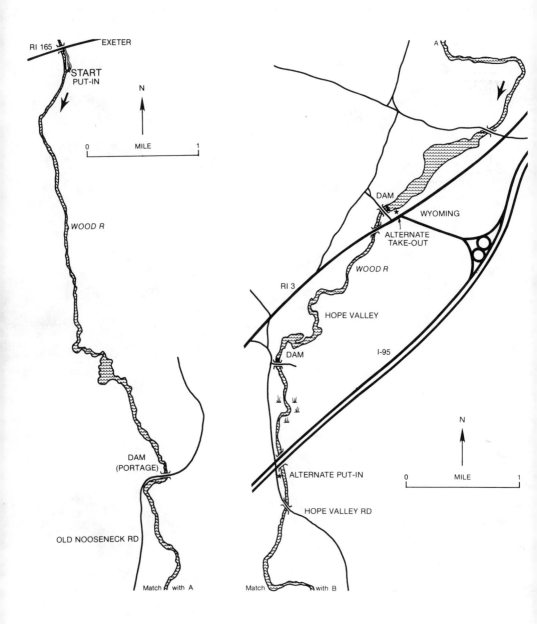

RI 165 — EXETER

START
PUT-IN

N

0 — MILE — 1

WOOD R

DAM
(PORTAGE)

OLD NOOSENECK RD

Match with A

A

DAM

WYOMING

ALTERNATE
TAKE-OUT

WOOD R

RI 3

HOPE VALLEY

DAM

I-95

ALTERNATE PUT-IN

HOPE VALLEY RD

Match with B

N

0 — MILE — 1

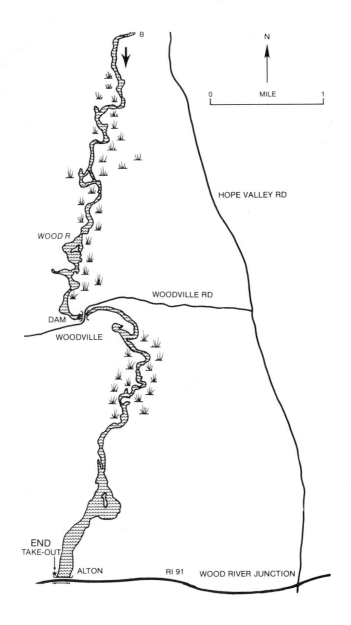

B

N

0   MILE   1

HOPE VALLEY RD

WOOD R

WOODVILLE RD

DAM

WOODVILLE

END
TAKE-OUT

ALTON   RI 91   WOOD RIVER JUNCTION

95 *Rhode Island*

next bridge, but access here is not good and there is another dam less than a mile ahead. Thus, you may want to skip this segment entirely and begin a new trip on the lower section of the Wood from the Hope Valley Road landing.

Hope Valley Road landing
The six miles from Hope Valley to Alton is the prettiest section of the Wood, and possibly the most delightful canoeing area in Rhode Island. The water is clear and the current moderate; the shores wooded and wild. You will run into deadwater above a dam at Woodville and again in the pond above Alton, but the rest of the way it's simply a matter of floating around the bends and enjoying the tranquility. As with most rivers, the Wood does change complexion with the seasons. Spring trips here are the easiest, for the water is high and there will be few obstacles in your path. In July or August, on the other hand, you may have to lift over logs and blowdowns that you would float over in April. The extra effort in early summer, however, is worthwhile because of the wealth of laurel blossoms that decorate the slopes.

Woodville Dam
Nearly the entire stretch from Hope Valley to the dam at Woodville is through forest, with laurel liberally sprinkled among the maples, oaks, and birches. However, the best blossom show lies far ahead. When you reach a little marsh with a string of houses on the left, you are nearing Woodville. The dam is just before the bridge; it is best to take out on the right side. To continue carry across the bridge and put in again on the left side. The river is wider here and more open, with white water lilies blooming in the shallows in summer. Shortly you will reach a fork. Turn left. The right fork, which has fooled many canoeists, shrinks to a little brook behind a farm.

It is barely an hour's paddle from Woodville to Alton, but during June and July this section fairly glows with laurel blossoms. The area just before you enter Alton Pond is best of all. Here the entire shore on the left is bedecked with towering laurel bushes. The dazzling pink and white blossoms come right down to the water; paddling over to them for a rest break is very hard to resist.

Alton Dam/ end
You may need that rest, too, once you round the point and enter Alton Pond, for when a headwind is blowing it can be difficult to paddle over the shallow but choppy water. Staying close to shore usually helps avoid some of the wind, but when the water is low you may have to travel the open channels. Aim for the right end of the dam. A concrete ramp is situated just before the dam and your car will be just above the ramp.

Pawcatuck River

Alton to Potter Hill

Put-in Points	Take-out Points	Approximate Distance	Approximate Trip Time	Condition of Water	Portages
Alton Dam	Bradford landing	5 miles	2½ hours	Smooth	None
Alton Dam	Potter Hill Dam	12¾ miles	5-5½ hours	Smooth	Bradford Dam

The Pawcatuck River in southwestern Rhode Island is for those who like their canoeing nice and easy. Flowing through attractive woodlands, the river is smooth and wide, with enough water for late summer and autumn trips. Because it holds its water well, and because the shoreline trees put on a dazzling foliage display in fall, the Pawcatuck should be saved for late-season canoeing. Pick a day when a slow and leisurely cruise is appealing, for there is little current here except during spring. Hurrying through these woods, with the trees ablaze with color, would be a shame anyway.

The lone exception to the generally quiet waters is a short stretch soon after you begin, where there is a broken dam that is runable. In addition, there is one portage on the route, a short carry around another dam. The rest of the way is smooth paddling.

Access

You can make a short trip (5 miles, 2½ hours) or a long trip (12¾ miles, 5 to 5½ hours) on the Pawcatuck. The longer run ends by a dam at Potter Hill a short distance north of Westerly. The take-out point is most easily reached by driving to the village of Ashaway on RI 3, turning west on RI 216 and shortly turning south on River Street. Follow River Street to the first bridge, which is just above the Potter Hill Dam. You can park just beyond the bridge beside the burned-out rubble of an old mill.

The shorter trip, with a take-out at Bradford, includes the faster water near the put-in at Alton and the broken dam run, but avoids the Bradford Dam portage. A state landing on RI 216 in Bradford makes a handy take-out if the 5-mile trip appeals to you.

To reach the put-in point, drive RI 216 (east from Ashaway, north from Bradford) to RI 91, which you then will follow north to Alton. Park in a lot at a state landing beside Alton Dam, and launch your canoe by carrying it accross the highway and down a steep bank to the river below the dam. This is actually the Wood River (see Trip 14) here. A short distance below the dam the Wood joins the Charles River to form the Pawcatuck.

The River

Start/
Alton
Dam

Just below Alton Dam, the Wood River has some current and is very shallow, but it soon opens into a smooth waterway. The Wood runs about ½ mile to its junction with the Charles, which comes in from the left. The combined waters assure you of easy floating the rest of the way. In very early spring, after heavy rains or sudden thaws, the section of the Pawcatuck just below the junction can be wild—even treacherous—but during summer and fall it is pleasant and sets the mood for the rest of the trip: nice and easy.

Both banks are wooded through this first stretch. You will pass a string of houses on the right, each home with its own dock. On the docks are metal benches, showing that the landowners here appreciate the relaxed mood of the river. In fall, you will see perhaps the best of the trip's foliage show in this area. Maple trees dominate the shorelines, creating an awesome display of orange, scarlet, and gold. Numerous pines are scattered about, too, and a wide variety of other trees and bushes will be noticed by canoeists who take their time paddling by.

When the shoreline vegetation on the left breaks open and reveals a large farm, you are nearing the community of Burdickville and the broken dam. When the current is slow—which is the case most of the time—you can safely paddle quite close to the jumbled stones of the dam for a look before going over. Easiest place to run it is at the extreme right, where a chute was recently installed beside a new retaining wall. In all but the driest times, you will run the rapid easily. A note of caution: watch for a metal rod extending from a stone beside the wall. Be sure to stay near the left side of the chute. Experienced canoeists also can run other sections of the original dam but both shores are posted and getting out for a lookover is difficult.

From the broken dam to Bradford you will paddle through about 2 miles of nearly unbroken woodland. You leave Burdickville heading south and will reach Bradford paddling north, for the river makes a big horseshoe-shaped curve. You will pass under a railroad bridge along one arm of the horseshoe and then later float beneath another bridge of the same railroad. There are no other bridges in this area, which is generally lowland. Shortly after passing the first railroad bridge, you will come to a well-worn sandy

Two couples put in below Bradford Dam.

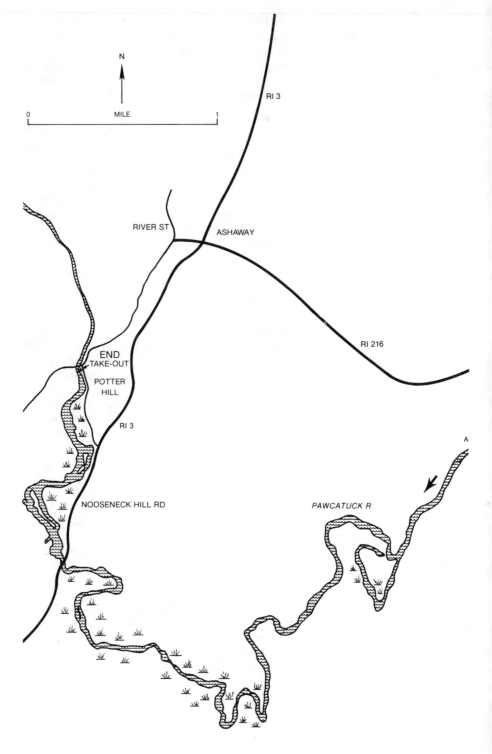

N

0   MILE   1

RI 3

RIVER ST

ASHAWAY

RI 216

END
TAKE-OUT

POTTER
HILL

RI 3

A

NOOSENECK HILL RD

PAWCATUCK R

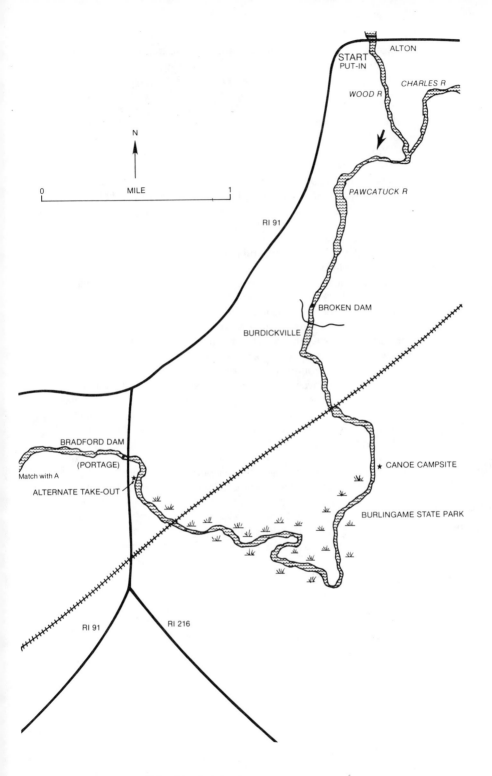

ALTON

START
PUT-IN

CHARLES R

WOOD R

PAWCATUCK R

N

0   MILE   1

RI 91

BROKEN DAM

BURDICKVILLE

BRADFORD DAM

(PORTAGE)

Match with A

ALTERNATE TAKE-OUT

★ CANOE CAMPSITE

BURLINGAME STATE PARK

RI 91   RI 216

101   *Rhode Island*

spot at the water's edge on the left. A path to the woods indicates much traffic in and out of the river. This spot is a canoe campsite in Burlingame State Park. Burlingame is Rhode Island's largest campground with more than 750 tent and trailer campsites, but this is the only area set aside for canoeists. It consists of just rock-ringed fire pits and enough room beneath the tall pines for tents, but it is a pretty spot for a rest break even on day trips.

You are likely to have company along this stretch of the river. Tree swallows and barn swallows swoop low over the water in pursuit of insects throughout the warmer months, and kingfishers will travel with you, screaming in protest, as they fly just ahead of the canoe for considerable distances. Fishermen, too, work this area, and you are likely to pass a number of small boats and anchored canoes as you near Bradford. If you are taking out at

Bradford landing Bradford, start looking for the landing on the left soon after you float under the second railroad bridge.

To continue to Potter Hill, paddle past the Bradford landing and under the RI 91 bridge to the Bradford Dam, which lies shortly beyond. The portage around the right end of the dam is short and easy. The 1971 Appalachian Mountain Club New England Canoeing Guide says this dam can be run, but don't try it. The drop is several feet onto jagged rocks; few canoes or their passengers are likely to come through undamaged. Below Bradford Dam, the river winds through lovely wild country, passing woods with tall trees, occasional swamps, and many acres of tangled marsh vegetation. It is not uncommon to see deer in the wooded areas. And ducks flock to the patches of swamp in the fall, accounting for the shooting blinds you pass. Before reaching the marshlands, you will come upon the stone abutments of a long-vanished bridge. The right side, grassy and shady, offers a perfect picnic site.

There is practically no current through the swamp. Thus it will take a good deal of paddling to reach the next landmark, the RI 3 bridge. Once past this bridge, it is less than a mile, through a stretch

Potter Hill Dam/end with houses on both shores, to the bridge above Potter Hill Dam. The take-out is best on the right, just before the bridge.

Trips in
Connecticut

Moosup River

Almyville to Central Village

Put-in Point	Take-out Point	Approximate Distance	Approximate Trip Time	Condition of Water	Portages
Almyville Dam	CT 14 bridge	3½ miles	2 hours	Rapids	3 or 4

If you are a flatwater canoeist, and want to see what whitewater paddling is all about, the Moosup River in eastern Connecticut is a good place to start. The river is short and not particularly dangerous, yet it offers enough rapids and rock dodging to get your feet wet—often literally—in an adventure-filled run.

The Moosup does have a couple of drawbacks. First, there are numerous dams in the 3½-mile trip described here. Three of them must be carried around. Two others, however, one-foot drops each, can be run. Also, there is a broken dam that can be shot if the water is high enough and the canoeists both confident and capable. You should plan for three short portages and possibly four.

Water depth is the other problem in this stretch of the Moosup. It can be run only in early spring. By summer you can walk across the stream at virtually any point. This usually means a trip in March when the water is extremely cold. If you are running this river, wear a wet suit or bring along dry clothing in a waterproof bag.

Still, the river is worth canoeing. It is nearly all rapids or riffles, mostly Class I and II according to the American Canoe Association ratings. The river is enough of a challenge to keep experienced canoeists interested, and yet easy enough so that beginners won't be dumped every few minutes. If you are a novice at quickwater canoeing, however, it is wise to team up with an old pro. At the very least, you should travel in a group with several other canoes, and by all means wear a life preserver for the entire trip. The Moosup is no wading pool; there have been tragic accidents on it.

If the water is high enough, you can run the broken dam before the first bridge.

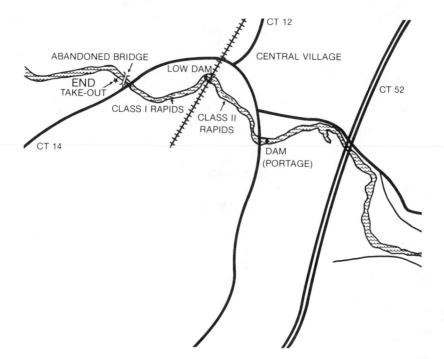

Access

The Moosup begins in Rhode Island, but the upper part is shallow, narrow, and often clogged with blowdowns and debris. The best canoeing section, therefore, is on the Connecticut side, from Almyville to the western edge of Central Village. To leave a car at take-out, drive to the CT 14 bridge in Central Village. On the west side of the river a road leads to an old, unused bridge. You can park along this road and take out just beyond the old bridge. You'll have to pull your canoe up a steep bank here, but this is the last take-out spot on the Moosup. Beyond this point, the river runs about 2 miles through farmland (a stretch in which there are more blowdowns than rapids) and then empties in to the Quinebaug River (see Trip 17). The first place to take out on the Quinebaug is 4 miles after the confluence, so if you run past this old bridge, you have to canoe 6 additional miles.

To reach put-in, drive east on CT 14 as it follows the river through

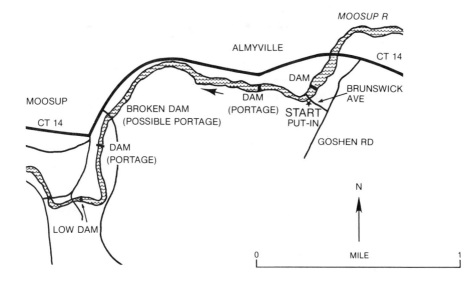

Central Village, Moosup and Almyville—giving you ample opportunity to scout the water by car—until crossing the river on the high CT 14 bridge. Turn right on the first road, Goshen Road, drive a few blocks to Brunswick Avenue, turn right again and park beside a barricaded old bridge just below a high dam. Launch on the left side of Brunswick Avenue.

The River

Start/
Almyville
Dam

After launching, you'll find the going easy for a short stretch that ends at the first dam. Carry around this dam on the right. Below it you'll hit riffles that occasionally grow into rapids. For the most part the rocks are small and just below the water's surface. Several boulder patches, however, give an indication of what is ahead. Throughout this stretch, CT 14 runs along on top of the high bank on the right, a comforting thought should your canoe swamp or other problems arise. In addition, you'll pass under numerous bridges, including one near every dam, so the chance of being stranded should your canoe get away from you is nonexistent.

Broken dam
One of the greatest challenges of this trip lies just before the first bridge. Here you'll find a broken dam with huge concrete slabs strewn across the river. You can, and should, pull out on the left for a good look, and you may want to portage. If the water is high enough, however, you can make an exciting run over the right end. Be sure you make a hard draw left just as you cascade into the standing waves. Even the best canoeists get splashed here, but most come through without major difficulties.

Dam
After a short rapid, the river calms considerably, a clue that another dam is just ahead. You should carry around this one on the right, near the mouth of an old mill canal, where you'll have to lift your canoe over a four-foot ledge. The river then runs narrow and shallow. Just before another bridge, you reach one of those low barriers. Most canoes will skim right over if not heavily loaded.

After this low dam, there is a long stretch of riffles, some requiring extensive backwatering and drawing maneuvers. You'll pass under two bridges and then the Connecticut Turnpike (CT 52) bridges on this segment and reach a pond created by still another dam. This one cannot be run—in 1977 a man lost his life trying.

Dam
Portage around either end of the dam. If you take out on the left, you can walk on a lane ahead to the CT 12 bridge and scout the rapids the most difficult so far. Class II or tougher, they consist of jumbled rocks scattered all over the riverbed, creating an obstacle course requiring considerable skill and teamwork. After you pass under the bridge, you will swirl around a bend and be greeted by more huge boulders. Fortunately, the current swings you toward the left shore, putting you on the best route through this hazardous section.

One more difficult area lies ahead. When you come to the next 1-foot dam, just beyond a railroad bridge, pull out on the left and walk ahead for a look at the section below. This long run of rapids is probably the most demanding of any on the river because total concentration is required. You'll have to pick your way through a zigzag course, and the careless sooner or later find themselves broadside to one of the boulders. When groups canoe this stretch of rapids, the leaders usually swing over to shore or into an eddy after making the run and watch as each succeeding canoe comes through. Even those who bounce off a few rocks along the way often get a cheer from their comrades on passing the test. For now they are whitewater canoeists.

CT 14 bridge/ end
The take-out spot is just a short distance ahead. You'll pass under two bridges in quick succession. After slipping over a ledge and a slight drop at the second bridge, pull over to the left bank. Those who got a little wet while shooting that last run of rapids will be glad the car is so near. Whitewater canoeing in March is fun, but it can be awfully cold.

17

Quinebaug River

Central Village to north of Jewett City

Put-in Point	Take-out Points	Approximate Distance	Approximate Trip Time	Condition of Water	Portages
CT 205	CT 14 bridge	6$^1/_2$ miles	2$^1/_2$ hours	Mostly smooth	None
CT 205	Butts Bridge Road bridge	11$^1/_2$ miles	4-4$^1/_2$ hours	Mostly smooth	None

Save the Quinebaug River for a day in midspring, after whitewater fever has subsided but before New England rivers slow to their summer pace. On a sparkling late April or May morning, the Quinebaug offers an easy cruise through an underrated area rich in both wildlife and scenic attractions.

The Quinebaug flows down the eastern edge of Connecticut until it joins the Shetucket (see Trip 18) just above Norwich to form the Thames. The upper reaches of the Quinebaug have long been harnessed for power, and numerous dams make canoeing that area difficult. In the stretch described here, however, you can enjoy a most pleasant 11$^1/_2$-mile float without a single portage. There are brief sections of quickwater shortly after the put-in, but the remainder of the trip is a smooth journey. The current is fast enough to require little paddling, yet calm enough to allow time to enjoy the surroundings.

Access

You have a choice of take-out points. You can end your trip at the CT 14 bridge a few miles west of Central Village, giving you a short journey of approximately 6$^1/_2$ miles that will last 2$^1/_2$ hours or less. This section includes the most attractive scenery along the river and runs through part of the 1,200-acre Quinebaug River-Bramwell Wildlife Refuge. If you prefer a longer trip, continue driving west on CT 14 to CT 169, turn left (south), and go about 4 miles to Butts Bridge Road. A left turn here and a short drive will take you back to the river. The take-out will be on the left bank, so cross the bridge and continue to the end of the guardrail, where you can find adequate parking space. Canoeing to this bridge stretches your trip to about

11$^1/_2$ miles and will take about 4 to 4$^1/_2$ hours—longer if you take a lunch break.

To reach put-in, drive east on CT 14 into Central Village, then turn left (north) on CT 12. When you reach Wauregan, go left again on CT 205 for a short distance to the river. Just before the bridge is a dirt lane running to the left to a launching spot. There is plenty of room to leave a car here.

The River

Start/
CT 205

At your start, the river is broad but very shallow. It remains this way for the first 1$^1/_2$ miles. The river holds its water well and can be canoed all year, although it tends to be scratchy in the early segments during drier times. The higher water level and the increased bird activity in mid-spring make that the ideal time for this trip.

You will notice the beauty of this river immediately. The shores are lovely with huge trees towering above—many hemlocks as well as beeches and pines. In addition, there are numerous magnificent old sycamores and lush thickets of mountain laurel. The blossoms of the laurel add a bonus for canoeists passing this area in late May or June.

In less than an hour after launching, you will pass a feeder stream entering quietly from the left. This is the Moosup River (see Trip 16), a very popular whitewater creek in March. Here, at its end, however, it is calm and unpretentious. Many canoeists on the Quinebaug don't even notice it. Nobody will miss the next feature, though, for just past the Moosup junction you come to perhaps the largest patch of rapids on this trip. It is easy—and prudent if you are not used to quickwater—to pull out on the right and walk ahead for a good look at the rapids. Carry around on the right, too, if the route appears too difficult or the water is too low. Usually this section can be run without trouble if you stay to the right of center.

After this quickwater, it is literally smooth sailing all the way. Take time to enjoy the wildlife. During spring, you will flush wood ducks, mallards, or black ducks at nearly every bend. Kingfishers will protest from perches above you, sandpipers will be probing the shoreline, and herons will be stalking through the shallows. In addition, songbirds will maintain a musical din in the woods. And you are likely to see a muskrat or two swim across the river ahead of your canoe.

As you near a sharp left turn in the river, you will hear what sounds like rapids. A number of boulders at the water's edge on the right create the noise but they present no problem if you stay to the

Once you pass the rapids below the confluence with the Moosup River, the Quinebaug is smooth paddling.

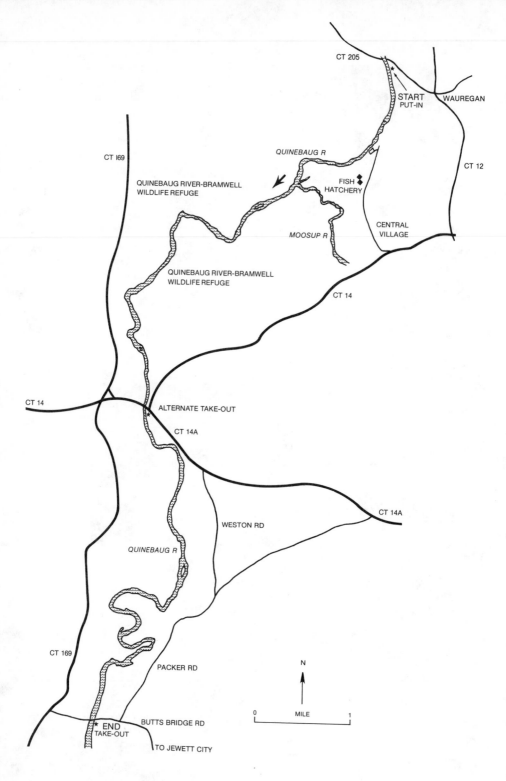

CT 205

START
PUT-IN

WAUREGAN

CT 169

QUINEBAUG R

CT 12

QUINEBAUG RIVER-BRAMWELL
WILDLIFE REFUGE

FISH
HATCHERY

MOOSUP R

CENTRAL
VILLAGE

QUINEBAUG RIVER-BRAMWELL
WILDLIFE REFUGE

CT 14

CT 14

ALTERNATE TAKE-OUT

CT 14A

CT 14A

WESTON RD

QUINEBAUG R

N

0   MILE   1

CT 169

PACKER RD

★ END
TAKE-OUT

BUTTS BRIDGE RD

TO JEWETT CITY

112   *Connecticut*

left, which is completely clear, as you swing around the bend. There are only a few other areas of minor riffles before you reach

CT 14 bridge

the CT 14 bridge, your take-out if you opted for the shorter trip. If you parked on the right, take out just before the bridge. if your car is on the left, go just past the bridge.

Those who continue canoeing to Butts Bridge Road will find even fewer riffles in this stretch. First there is a high, rocky ridge decorated with hemlock and laurel on the right shore, but soon the banks flatten into farm fields, most of which are screened from the river by trees. The Quinebaug then meanders through a broad flood plain. It is interesting to note just how high the shoreline trees are scarred from being struck by ice and debris during the late winter floods. There are no houses along the river here and the scenery, while not as spectacular as along the first part of the trip, remains pleasant except for the few minutes it takes to pass a landfill on the left.

Wildlife is abundant here as well. Crows call from the tall trees, red-winged blackbirds sing from the farm fields, and there are as many ducks here as in the protected area upriver. The high banks, again covered with hemlock and laurel, return, restoring the wilderness atmosphere to the river.

Butts Bridge Road bridge/ end

The first bridge you reach beyond the CT 14 bridge is your take-out point. Go just beyond the bridge and pull out on the left. Be careful to follow the path directly up to the road. All of the adjoining property is another wildlife refuge, and trespassing is not permitted. Obey the signs. Your courtesy will help keep the Quinebaug pleasant for canoeists for many years to come.

Shetucket River

South Windham to Baltic

Put-in Point	Take-out Point	Approximate Distance	Approximate Trip Time	Condition of Water	Portages
CT 203 bridge	CT 97 bridge	7¾ miles	3-3½ hours	Smooth early, then riffles	Scotland Dam

In eastern Connecticut, canoeists seeking whitewater usually head for the Salmon River (see Trip 20) or the Moosup River (see Trip 16), while those preferring flatwater go to the Quinebaug (see Trip 17). Not as well known, but located in the same general area, is the Shetucket River; it offers both kinds of water. The quickwater is more on the order of riffles than rapids, but under the right conditions, it provides a taste of what rock dodging is all about. There are no dangerous spots—just scattered patches of boulders with plenty of room to maneuver your canoe. The flatwater segment of this trip—the first 3 miles or so—is almost mirror smooth. Family groups and less-experienced canoeists should be able to handle this journey with little difficulty.

What splits the Shetucket into virtually two separate rivers is the huge Scotland Dam. The dam must be portaged, but the carry is not difficult and it is the only one on this trip. The total distance of the trip is about 7¾ miles; normally it will take about 3½ hours. A strong headwind on the pondlike stretch above the dam or extremely low water with lots of bottom scraping below the dam, however, will slow you down considerably. Both factors should be considered before starting out.

Access

Put-in is at the CT 203 bridge at the village of South Windham, just downriver from Willimantic. You will take out at the CT 97 bridge in Baltic. Access is not particularly easy at either end. Be prepared to carry your canoe and gear a few yards farther than on most of the trips described in this book. At Baltic, drive to a large parking area just east of the bridge, and leave your car in the extreme right corner of the lot. A footpath follows the river about 100 feet farther to the right, and ends at a suitable landing in a wooded area. It is possible to take out closer to your car, but if you do you will have to

Once past this large squarish boulder you will be nearing the end of your trip.

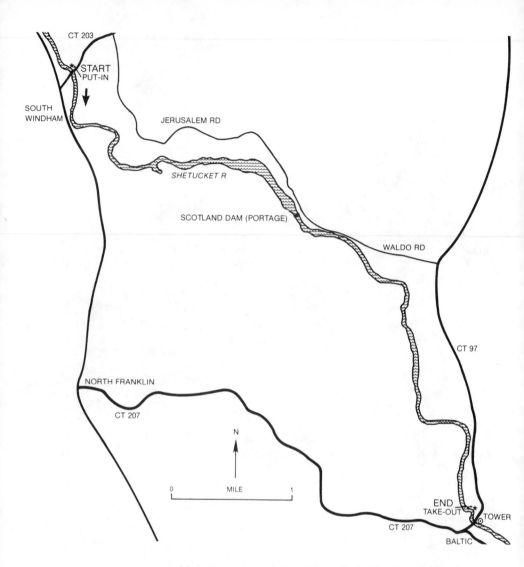

cope with a stronger current and then climb a steep, stony bank.

To reach the put-in pick up CT 207 just west of the bridge at take-out, follow it west 5 miles to North Franklin, then take CT 32 north 3 miles to CT 203. The bridge over the Shetucket is a short distance to your right on CT 203. There is ample parking east of the bridge at an electric power plant, but your canoe will have to be carried back to the bridge and then down a path angling off the north side of the road. Launch beneath a big hickory tree.

The River

Start/ CT 203 bridge

Once on the river, you are likely to forget the problems you met launching. There is some current in this area, but the river is wide and smooth, with tall trees on both sides. Dense stands of hemlock contrast pleasantly with the lighter green of birches, maples, beeches, and oaks. Ferns, laurel, and other undergrowth is abundant, and at times moss-covered ledges rise above the shorelines. The forest is virtually unbroken all the way to the dam. If there is a headwind, paddle close to shore. The right bank offers the most protection and also has the better scenery. After a few bends and as the river grows wider, you will notice some landmarks on the left shore—a picnic pavilion, railroad tracks, and a few cottages perched at the water's edge. When you pass the cottages, you are nearing the Scotland Dam, so stay along the right shore. You will see a brick maintenance building at the left end of the dam as you round a bend. If you are already floating along the right bank, you

Scotland Dam should have no problem in easing up to the right end. This dam is one of the more elaborate of those canoeists encounter in southern New England. It is controlled by computers that calculate power requirements, so the amount of water it releases varies considerably.

Re-entering the river requires a carry across the dike at the dam's right end and down past a pile of jagged stones. You can launch here in a quiet eddy and then take a good look back at the dam, now towering above you, before swinging out into the current. Even with the increased current, the river remains quite smooth for ¼ mile or so. Then, just as you pass a feeder stream coming in from the left, you reach the riffles. Water depth determines the number of rocks you can float over and those that must be avoided, but slipping past these obstacles is usually easy and fun. The current is good—normally you can float the 4½ miles from the Scotland Dam to Baltic in about 1½ to 2 hours. This stretch is a delightful change of pace after the flatwater earlier in the trip. The river remains wide, and rocks and riffles combine with wooded banks to create a feeling that you are in some wilderness setting rather than midway between the cities of Willimantic and Norwich. Soon after passing a cabin in a clearing on the right, the river makes a sweeping curve to the right. Stay along the right shore to remain in the best channel. The left side is very shallow. For some distance here, brief periods of calm water alternate with long stretches of "bumpy" water—that is, minor riffles and good, fast current. You will reach one section in which large boulders are strewn across the river. It looks difficult from a distance, but there is plenty of room for you to float by.

After passing a large squarish rock in midriver, you will have completed the most noteworthy stretches. A few more riffles and an insignificant boulder patch lie ahead, followed by a few minutes of paddling in smooth water. When the high stone tower of a mill

CT 97 bridge/ end building looms into view, prepare to move out of the current to the left. The landing spot is on the outside of a curve, just above another set of riffles and the CT 97 bridge.

Willimantic River

Stafford Springs to Willimantic

Put-in Point	Take-out Points	Approximate Distance	Approximate Trip Time	Condition of Water	Portages
CT 32 bridge	Eagleville Dam	14½ miles	5 hours	Fast, mostly riffles	None
CT 32 bridge	CT 31 bridge	17½ miles	6 hours	Fast, riffles, last stretch smooth	Eagleville Dam

The Willimantic River east of Hartford is ideal for canoeists who want to try quickwater for the first time, or perhaps brush up their rock-dodging skills before tackling some of the wilder rivers of New England. This stretch of the Willimantic offers 5 or 6 hours (depending on where you take out) of delightful floating through a scenic, wooded valley. The river is known for its natural beauty, its fishing, and its rocks. For most of this trip you won't have much time to admire the leafy shorelines—you'll be too busy steering your way around rocks in the stream and trying to read the next batch of riffles. The water is shallow virtually all the way, and about the only danger is the possibility of scratching or maybe denting your canoe.

Access

The most popular run on the Willimantic is from Stafford Springs to Eagleville Dam, a distance of about 14½ miles. To leave a car at the dam, drive CT 32 to Eagleville, which is about 6 miles north of the city of Willimantic, and turn west on CT 275. There is parking space on both ends of the dam. You can add 3 miles and an hour to your trip by taking out beside the CT 31 bridge, also just a short distance west of CT 32. In driving to the put-in point, follow CT 32 north until

Shallow and rock-strewn, the Willimantic is ideal for canoeists who want to try quickwater for the first time.

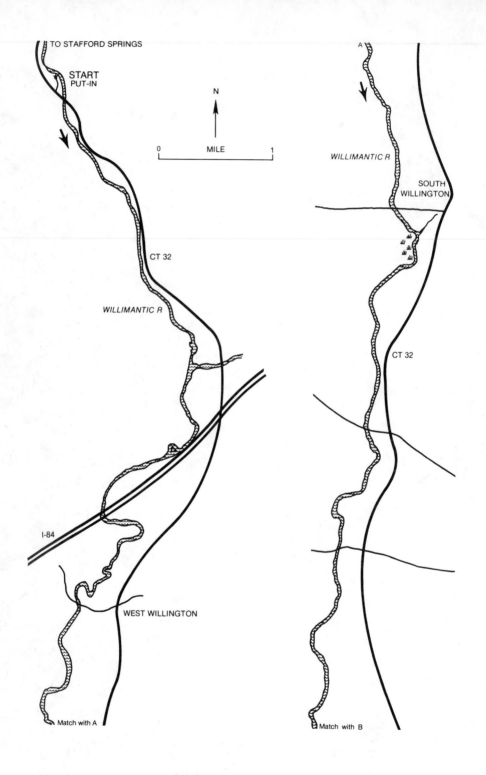

TO STAFFORD SPRINGS

START
PUT-IN

N

0   MILE   1

CT 32

WILLIMANTIC R

I-84

WEST WILLINGTON

Match with A

A

WILLIMANTIC R

SOUTH
WILLINGTON

CT 32

Match with B

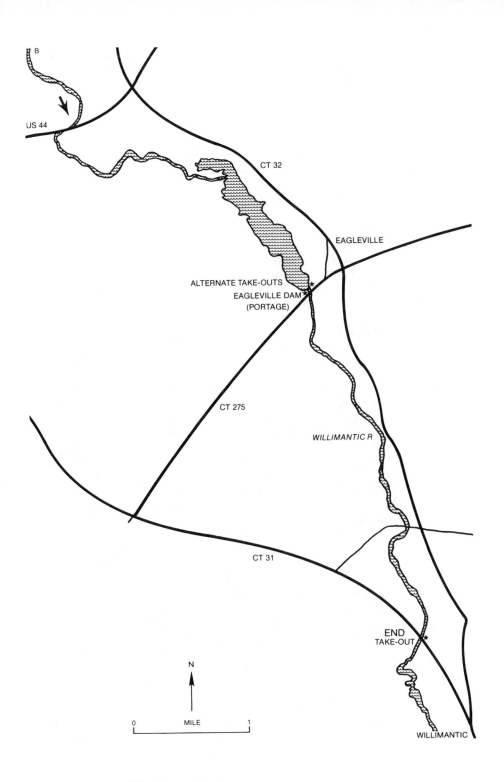

B

US 44

CT 32

EAGLEVILLE

ALTERNATE TAKE-OUTS
EAGLEVILLE DAM
(PORTAGE)

CT 275

WILLIMANTIC R

CT 31

END
TAKE-OUT

N

0   MILE   1

WILLIMANTIC

121 *Connecticut*

it crosses the river 2$\frac{1}{2}$ miles beyond the I-84 overpass. A narrow side road winds downhill beside the CT 32 bridge to a launching site.

The River

At the start, the river is narrow, fast, and loud, gurgling over thousands of rocks. These conditions are a good indication of what lies ahead, for although the river widens as it flows south, these little rapids continue until you reach the deadwater above Eagleville Dam. A look at the larger rocks in the water near the put-in shows just how popular this river is with canoeists. Nearly every stone carries scrape marks—red, green, or yellow paint, or the white scars left by aluminum canoes. But even this upper portion can be canoed with some care and skill. You may occasionally nudge a submerged rock unseen in the dark water, but for the most part winding your way through the maze is not only possible but very enjoyable. If you do run aground, it's usually a simple matter for the stern man to step out into the water and float the canoe a few feet to deeper water.

After paddling slightly less than an hour, all through these shallow riffles, you will pass a brook entering from the left. At this point, the river becomes wider and smoother, and you'll get a breather from your rock dodging. Now you can take in the hemlocks, birches, laurel, and maples that decorate the river's banks, effectively screening you from nearly all houses and roadways. But don't be fooled into thinking the riffles are finished. After just a brief respite, you will come to many more, some of which are punctuated by big boulders scattered haphazardly across the river. There is, however, more water and it is easier to maneuver around the obstacles here than earlier.

Stone abutments from vanished bridges offer picturesque spots for rest breaks or picnics, or you may want to stop in this area and try the fishing. The upper Willimantic is stocked heavily with trout; you are likely to meet fishermen here on any spring trip. Only fly fishing is permitted and all fish caught must be released. Shortly after passing under the I-84 bridges, you will enter a valley. Breaks in the shoreline foliage reveal lush farmlands. One minute you'll feel far removed from all civilization, alone with the birdsong and tumbling river, and the next, you will be treated to the aroma of new-mown hay or find yourself being stared at by a herd of cattle.

In about 2 hours (5 miles) from your start, you will reach the Willington Bridge; the next few miles are marked by several more bridges. Throughout this stretch, the water is fairly smooth, with just enough rocks and riffles to keep it interesting. The current remains steady, and practically no paddling is required between the short stretches of quickwater. Eventually, the current slows and the river opens as you near the Eagleville Dam. Long before you can see the dam itself, you will become aware of its presence by the slower current and by the thick growths of water lilies and pickerel-weeds.

Eagleville Dam

The reservoir created by the dam takes some work to cross—as do all such ponds. If the dam is your take-out point, aim for the side on which you parked your car. If you are continuing to the CT 31 take-out, however, head for the dam's right side. It offers a much better portage and re-entry. Below the dam and for the last few miles to CT 31, the river is quite fast and meanders much more than the earlier stretches. There are still occasional rocks to dodge, but not many. This portion is generally an easy and relaxing hour's ride through delightful woodland. It's especially pretty in June when the mountain laurel is in bloom.

CT 31 bridge/ end

Be careful, though, that you don't become so relaxed that you float right by your take-out point. The CT 31 bridge, unmarked from the river, is a modern steel structure considerably higher on the left than on the right. Another significant landmark is a stone retaining wall on the left, just before the bridge and below the parking area and your car.

Salmon River

West of Colchester to near Westchester

Put-in Point	Take-out Point	Approximate Distance	Approximate Trip Time	Condition of Water	Portages
River Road bridge	Old Comstock Bridge	3½ miles	2-2½ hours	Rapids	None

For many canoeists in southern New England, spring would not be complete without a run on the Salmon River in south central Connecticut. Traffic on the Salmon can be heavy in late March and early April as whitewater enthusiasts swarm in from Hartford and the University of Connecticut to the north, Rhode Island to the east, and the New York City area to the southwest. Not many leave the Salmon disappointed.

The Salmon is definitely a whitewater river. It consists of continuous rapids and should not be attempted by novices unless accompanied by experienced canoeists. Even the very best canoeists should keep safety uppermost in mind. Go in a group, take extra paddles, wear life jackets, and if at all possible, wear wet suits—the water is extremely cold in March. It is a rare canoeist indeed who can negotiate all the maneuvers and obstacles on this stretch of river without getting wet.

Several segments of the Salmon and the two smaller rivers that form it, the Blackledge and the Jeremy, can be canoed, but the section described here is the most popular. This is a short stretch, barely 3½ miles long, but it is 3½ miles of quickwater and rapids rated Class II and III by the American Canoe Association and the Appalachian Mountain Club. In moderately high water, there are no portages except, perhaps, for a broken dam near the end. And even the dam can be run by the more adventurous. In fact, for many it is the highlight of the trip.

Water depth, the key in any whitewater canoeing, is especially critical on the Salmon, where the rapids and their degree of difficulty change constantly. One rainstorm, for example, can

This stretch of the Salmon is for those who have already learned how to dodge rocks!

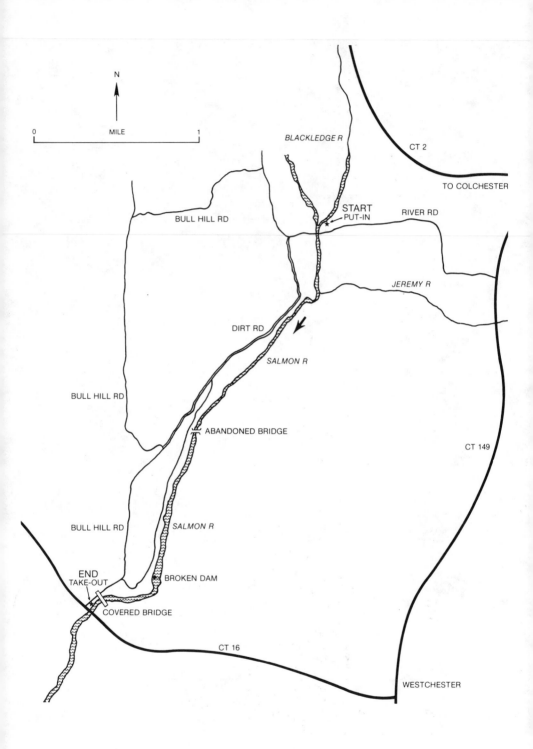

mean the difference between an exhilarating dash down the river and a day spent scratching bottom on a thousand rocks.

Access

The best route to take-out is CT 2 to Exit 16 a few miles west of Colchester. That exit puts you on CT 149, which you then follow south to Ct 16 in Westchester. Turn right and drive a few miles to the river. Just upstream from the CT 16 bridge is a picturesque wooden covered bridge called the Old Comstock Bridge. This bridge and a nearby parking area make for a convenient take-out. Look over the water's depth here; this is possibly the most shallow segment of the trip. If the water flowing over the countless rocks beneath the covered bridge appears deep enough for a canoe, chances are there will be plenty of water for running the rapids upstream. If many of these rocks are exposed, you may be spending as much time dragging the canoe as paddling it.

To reach the put-in on the Blackledge River just above the beginning of the Salmon proper, you have some choices. You can follow Bull Hill Road, which runs by the covered bridge, on its roundabout way north to River Road, or you can take a dirt road that branches off to the right from Bull Hill Road and follows the river. In dry periods, the dirt road is quite passable and allows you to get a good look at the rapids you'll be shooting. In mud season, though, it's best to take the long way around. You'll get there quicker. You can also reach River Road by retracing your route on CT 16 and CT 149. The best put-in is on the upstream side of the east end of the River Road bridge.

The River

Start/
River
Road
bridge

The Blackledge here is quite shallow for the first half mile or so. When it is joined by the Jeremy coming in from the left, you will be on the Salmon. Here, both the rapids and the fun begin. Big boulders dot the riverbed and hundreds of other rocks lurk at or near the surface. You will find yourself hurtling through a spectacular valley whose walls are blanketed with hemlocks, but don't spend too much time looking around. Keep your eyes on the rocks and be prepared to do a lot of backwatering, drawing, and sweeping. Veteran canoeists say you cannot think about dodging the rocks one at a time; you have to think three of four maneuvers ahead. If you don't, you just might make a terrific move around one set of boulders and find yourself broadside to the next one.

The time estimate given for this trip, 2 to 2½ hours, can be reduced by making a straight, continuous run. Most canoeists do this river in groups, however, and it is a common practice for group leaders to pull over to shore after each patch of rapids to make certain all the other canoes have made the run successfully. This is a good safety procedure. It would be a mistake anyway to hurry through the Salmon River experience. It is better to savor the fun.

There are three major sets of rapids before you reach the first landmark, an old unused bridge roughly halfway to your take-out. Shortly after passing this bridge, you will float into a section with continuous riffles but fewer big rocks. Here the river widens a bit. In late March, the Salmon could use a traffic light in this area. In addition to all the groups going downstream, there are numerous single canoes and kayaks on the water. Many of these are competitors practicing on a slalom course in preparation for a number of races held every spring.

Just beyond this wide area, and heard before seen, is the washed-out dam and the foaming, frothing falls over the ledge rocks that remain. A high stone foundation on the right shore still clearly marks the spot. It is wise to pull out and walk ahead for a good look at what is in store. If you doubt your canoeing or swimming ability, carry around this falls. No momentary thrill is worth risking a tragedy. The falls can be run, however, through a deep chute that cuts through the ledge at the extreme right, just below your scouting position on the foundation. Once through the chute, you will drop into a pool and then you must make a quick left turn over a much smaller falls. If you take in a lot of water in the chute, just pull over to the right bank and empty your canoe before leaving the pool.

And don't forget to look over the falls before trying it. The last time we were there, two canoes approached where we were scouting the chute. The young couples paddling the canoes obviously had no intention of pulling ashore and ignored our calls. The first canoe, luckily, slipped over the falls successfully. The second one swamped. The canoe went down, and the two occupants got soaked. They were wearing neither life preservers nor wet suits, and they had to be helped from the icy water. It's likely they will show a bit more respect for the falls the next time around.

Old Comstock Bridge/ end   After the broken-dam falls, there are several stretches of riffles and a ledge or two on which heavily loaded canoes can get hung up. In less than ½ mile, however, you will come to the covered bridge and your take-out.

Lower Farmington River
Farmington to Weatogue

Put-in Point	Take-out Point	Approximate Distance	Approximate Trip Time	Condition of Water	Portages
CT 4 landing	CT 185 bridge	9½ miles	3½-4 hours	Smooth	None

In most canoeing books, the stretch of the Farmington River running from Farmington to Weatogue, just west of Hartford, is usually covered in one sentence. One guide popular with New England sportsmen dismisses the entire area with 14 words: "Here the river turns north and there is a fair current but no quickwater." It deserves far more attention.

As with the Housatonic River (see Trips 24 and 25), the Farmington offers you a choice. You can go a few miles northwest and do the upper Farmington (see Trip 22) with its rocky riffles, trout pools, and forested shorelines. Or you can stay closer to Hartford and do the lower Farmington, a relaxing 9½-mile float through an attractive valley. Along this portion of the river you'll see a surprisingly large variety of wildlife, pass by several golf courses and extensive tobacco fields, enjoy views of Talcott Mountain and Hueblein Tower, look for King Philip's Cave high on a ridge above the river, and finally take out beside one of the largest and most impressive trees in Connecticut.

The trip is ideal for family groups for there are no portages, rapids, or obstacles of any kind. And unlike the upper Farmington, which runs too shallow during the summer and fall for pleasant canoeing, this stretch usually can be run throughout the year.

Access

Access is easy. To leave a car at take-out, drive on CT 185 to where it crosses the Farmington in the Weatogue section of Simsbury. At the east end of the bridge, Nod Road breaks off to the south; there is a large parking area beside the river just a few yards down this road. For a more aesthetic take-out, however, follow a lane that goes north off CT 185. This lane leads to another large parking area dominated by an immense sycamore tree. A stone marker at its base identifies the tree as the Pinchot Sycamore and reveals its circumference—23 feet, 7 inches. The tree is named for Gifford Pinchot of Simsbury, who was the first chief of the U.S. Forestry Service.

Put-in is off CT 4 just above the town of Farmington. You can take Nod Road from CT 185 south to Avon, or you can cross the river and follow CT 10-US 202 to Avon, where you bear left onto US 44 briefly and cross the river. Then continue south on CT 10-US 202 until you arrive at CT 4. Go right on CT 4, and immediately after crossing the bridge, turn left down a lane to the landing. You'll find plenty of parking room.

The River

Start/
CT 4
landing

This valley is quite heavily settled and industrialized, but you would never know it from traveling on the river. For the most part, large trees line both shores and high banks blot out roads, buildings, and other signs of "civilization." The early going is somewhat typical of the entire trip. Tall maples, sycamores, and oaks shade the wide and smooth river. In addition, you'll notice a liberal sprinkling of mountain laurel, honeysuckle, and dogwood, all easy to spot in May when they are in bloom. Many of the stately old trees clinging to the banks are undercut. Occasionally, you'll come across trees that have fallen into the water, but the river is so wide there are no problems in swinging around them.

There is a golf course on the right shore at your start, then one on the left. Later, you will pass two more, one just beyond the bridge at Avon and another shortly before take-out. The trip, however, is not all golf courses. There are many areas of woods. In fact, you'll probably see more wildlife on this trip than on the upper Farmington even though that area more closely resembles what most people call "wilderness." There, heavy use by canoeists, fishermen, campers, and hikers scares off many of the animals and birds. In addition, what is there is often overlooked because canoeing quickwater doesn't leave much time for looking around.

Here, however, it is a different matter. Let the current do the work and enjoy your surroundings. Gray squirrels and chipmunks are abundant along the shorelines. So are orioles, cardinals, and chickadees. Swallows and kingbirds swoop over the water. Sandpipers dance along the mudflats. Kingfishers call from their perches. Woodchucks are often seen waddling along the banks and muskrats frequently swim ahead of your canoe. Raccoon tracks can be found on any sandbar, and often deer tracks, too. On one May trip on this stretch, we even came across two gray fox kits playing outside their den.

You come to the busy US 44 strip in Avon, approximately 6 miles from the starting point, in 2 to 2½ hours. Here, after leaving an extensive golf course behind, you'll come abreast of the tobacco

Here the Farmington is so placid that reflections are nearly mirror-perfect.

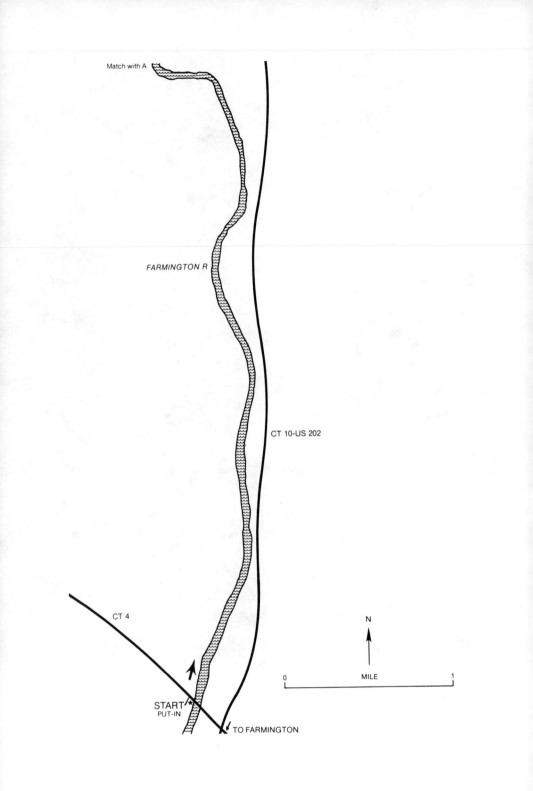

Match with A

FARMINGTON R

CT 10-US 202

CT 4

N

0   MILE   1

START
PUT-IN

TO FARMINGTON

132 *Connecticut*

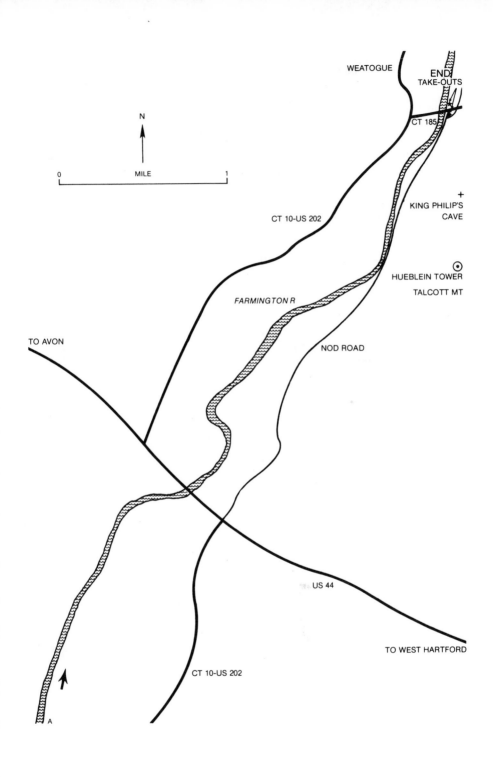

WEATOGUE

END
TAKE-OUTS

CT 185

N

0   MILE   1

+ KING PHILIP'S CAVE

CT 10-US 202

⊙ HUEBLEIN TOWER

TALCOTT MT

FARMINGTON R

TO AVON

NOD ROAD

US 44

TO WEST HARTFORD

CT 10-US 202

A

fields. Unfortunately, the high banks—a blessing elsewhere—are a drawback along this stretch because they prevent good views of the interesting tobacco farms with their screened fields and huge drying barns. In many cases, all you'll be able to see of the farms from the river are pumps that carry water to the fields. The high banks also make it difficult to find good picnic spots in this area.

Talcott Mountain, however, is high enough to be seen over the banks. It extends along your right for the rest of the journey. The most interesting feature on the ridge is the Heublein Tower, built by the Heublein family of cocktail fame. Long Island Sound can be seen from the tower on a clear day. As you view it from the river, the tower resembles a blunt-nosed rocket poised for take-off.

CT 185 bridge/ end

Keep an eye on the tower, for just about the time you pull even with it, the river bends to the right and the bow of your canoe will be pointing directly toward a stony knoll at the northern end of the Talcott Mountain ridge. Look closely, and you'll be able to see a rectangular hole. This is the cave from which the Indian chief, King Philip, supposedly directed the burning of Simsbury, just down the river, in 1676. Today the cave overlooks peaceful farms and one more golf course. When you come upon the golf course's parking lot on the right shore, your trip is nearly over. Look for the CT 185 bridge looming above. The take-out, whether you chose the Nod Road landing or left a car on the other side of the bridge beside the Pinchot Sycamore, is on the right.

Upper Farmington River

Riverton to Satan's Kingdom

Put-in Point	Take-out Points	Approximate Distance	Approximate Trip Time	Condition of Water	Portages
Riverton picnic area	CT 318 bridge	4½ miles	2 hours	Minor rapids, smooth stretches	None
Riverton picnic area	Above US 44 bridge	9½ miles	4-4½ hours	Minor rapids, some smooth stretches, riffles	None

Perhaps no stretch of any river in southern New England gets as much attention from outdoor enthusiasts in springtime as the upper reaches of the Farmington. While fishermen wade into the water or cast from the banks, and hikers, campers, and picnickers prowl the shorelines, there is often a steady flow of adventurers floating down the river in canoes, kayaks, rubber rafts, and even rubber inner tubes. There's good reason for the popularity of this segment of the Farmington, which lies in north central Connecticut. The water is clean and fast, and there are numerous calm pools. The banks are covered with relatively unspoiled forests, yet there are roads for easy access, and facilities for picnicking and camping. Also, the area's proximity to Hartford makes it readily available to large numbers of people who seek a day in the "wilderness."

The stretch described here runs about 9½ miles from Riverton to the US 44 bridge just above the famed gorge in the area between New Hartford and Canton called Satan's Kingdom. It is almost ideal from the canoeist's point of view. There is enough quickwater to make it challenging, and enough flatwater for relaxing breathers. There are islands to negotiate, and one set of rapids that requires some whitewater skill. Yet, under normal water conditions for April and May, there is little real danger. Except for Satan's Kingdom, that is.

This gorge lies a short distance below the US 44 bridge, so unless you are an accomplished whitewater canoeist, or you are traveling by rubber raft, watch your river landmarks carefully.

This crew gets a little help in one of the more shallow spots.

Access

Plan on taking out at a picnic area just off US 44 above the bridge. And when you leave a car here, note the landmarks along the river—a huge rock in the center of the river and an uprooted tree along the right shore. It may be difficult to pull out of the current if you go beyond these landmarks and pass under the bridge.

To reach put-in, take US 44 north to CT 181, and then follow CT 181 north along the river all the way to CT 20 at Riverton. (For most of this section, there is a road running along the other side of the river also, so it is easy to scout the water by car before launching.) The best put-in at Riverton is from a state picnic area just west of the CT 20 bridge, across the highway from the well-known Hitchcock Chair Factory.

The River

Start/
Riverton
picnic
area

The early going on the river is apt to be quite scratchy, with the best passage on the far right. Soon you'll begin what will become a familiar pattern, periods of rock dodging followed by flat pools. Riffles and pools alternate throughout much of this journey, with neither lasting more than a few minutes at a time. You may also have to dodge fishing lines, for trout anglers flock to this area in spring in quest of the brown, brook, and rainbow trout that are stocked several times during the season. You will pass a popular picnic area on the left, part of Peoples State Forest, and a less-visible recreation area on the right, the campground of American Legion State Forest. This campground is worth remembering if you are coming from any distance and plan to do the Lower Farmington (see Trip 21) the next day.

After passing between old stone footbridge abutments, you will enter a pretty section featuring good patches of riffles and shorelines of hemlocks, birches, and laurel. You won't be able to see any roads from the water, but they run close to the river on both sides here, a comforting thought in case of a spill or some other problem. The first of many islands appears in this stretch; most can be skirted on either side. As a general rule in the early going, however, the right passages are shallower and wider, the left faster and rockier. As always, if you are new to quickwater canoeing, play it safe and keep to the right.

The only rapid of any real concern is a stretch of boulders just after the river makes a curve to the left. A stand of tall straight pines on the left bank serves as a warning as you approach the bend. The rapid, considered Class II or III in American Canoe Association ratings, is difficult to negotiate cleanly, but you are more likely to get hung up than dumped into the water. In times of high water, of course, the complexion of the river changes considerably. At those times, only experts should be out on this stretch of the river.

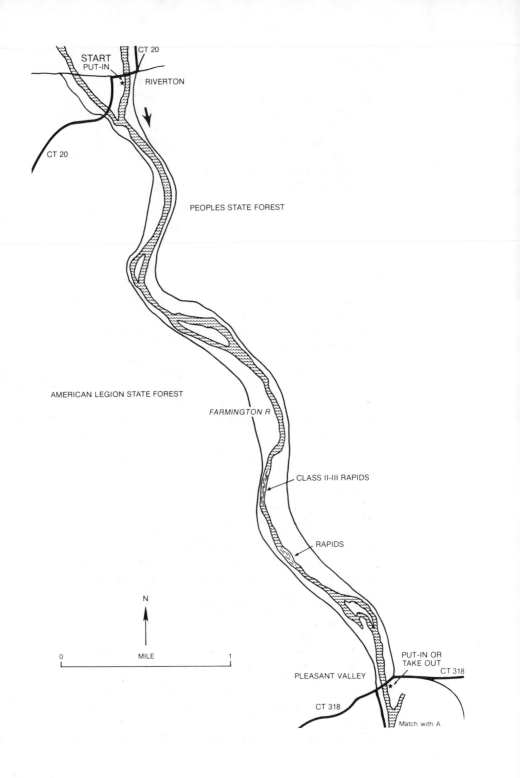

START
PUT-IN
CT 20
RIVERTON

CT 20

PEOPLES STATE FOREST

AMERICAN LEGION STATE FOREST

FARMINGTON R

CLASS II-III RAPIDS

RAPIDS

N

0   MILE   1

PUT-IN OR
TAKE OUT
CT 318

PLEASANT VALLEY

CT 318

Match with A

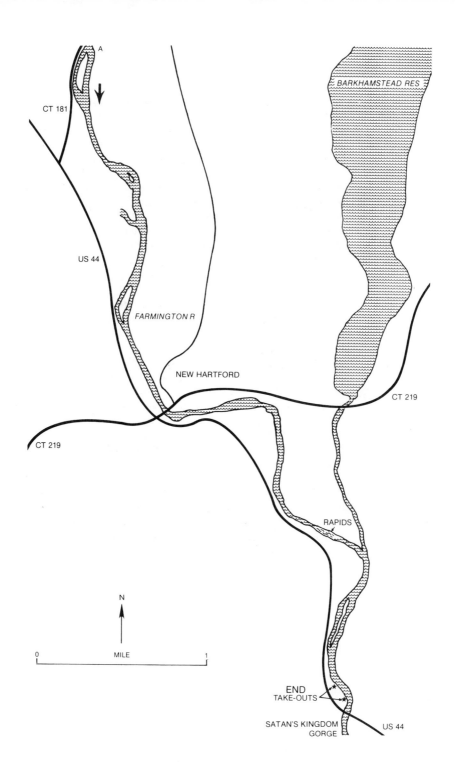

A

CT 181

US 44

FARMINGTON R

BARKHAMSTEAD RES

NEW HARTFORD

CT 219

CT 219

RAPIDS

N

0 MILE 1

END
TAKE-OUTS

SATAN'S KINGDOM
GORGE

US 44

The first bridge you pass under is the iron span for CT 318—about 4½ miles or roughly 2 hours from put-in. This area is the community of Pleasant Valley. There is a small put-in/take-out spot a short distance below the bridge on the left. From here to the next bridge, CT 219 at New Hartford, about 2½ miles downriver, the going is smoother with more flatwater than riffles. It takes only about 45 minutes to reach the CT 219 bridge, beyond which you again encounter minor rapids and riffles.

Just past the bridge, in an area dominated by a high retaining wall on the right, the river is wide and rocky, and care must be taken in zigzagging between the boulders. Rock dodging is the name of the game here. The rocks aren't large, but they are big enough to give you and your canoe a good jolt if you hit them. Keep in mind also, as you leave New Hartford behind, that the next bridge is US 44. If you miss it, you'll go into the gorge at Satan's Kingdom, so start looking now for the landmarks that will tell you how close you are getting.

Among the first buildings on the right shore will be a greenhouse and the Six D's Restaurant. In just a few minutes more, the buildings of the River Run Apartments will appear on the right. This is the time to ease up on your paddling and watch the water ahead more closely. As soon as you spot the large boulder (among many smaller ones) in midstream and the uprooted tree on the right, swing to the rightout of the current. You can land just behind the fallen tree. If you pass these markers and find yourself within sight of the high bridge, pull over to the right immediately. There is another landing here, on a point a short distance upstream from the bridge. This is the last good take-out spot before going into the gorge.

After landing, take a few minutes and follow a footpath under the bridge and along the river into Satan's Kingdom. High ledges tower above the water on both sides, and the river foams through a rocky chute. It's a splendid scene well worth the walk. But don't try taking a canoe through here. Leave that adventure for the rubber raft and inner tube enthusiasts.

Shepaug

Washington Depot to Roxbury Station

Put-in Point	Take-out Point	Approximate Distance	Approximate Trip Time	Condition of Water	Portages
CT 47 bridge	CT 67	8 miles	3-3½ hours	Riffles, minor rapids	None

Fantastic scenery, miles of fast, clean water, and no dams or portages—that's the Shepaug River. Possibly the most beautiful run in this book, or in all of southern New England for that matter, a trip down the Shepaug just might spoil you for tamer, less aesthetic outings. This river lies a long way from southern New England's major population centers, being hidden in the ancient hills of western Connecticut, but it's worth the drive to get there. Every canoeist with any quickwater skill at all should do the Shepaug at least once.

For the entire trip described here, an 8-mile stretch running from Washington Depot to a roadside park just north of Roxbury Station, the Shepaug offers riffles and minor rapids. This run is challenging enough to be fun, but not quite wild enough to be dangerous. And that's good, too, because for most of the trip the river runs through a stunning valley carved out of stone. At times the cliffs tower several hundred feet above you. With this scenery to look at, it can be difficult to concentrate on the water. Unfortunately, the Shepaug is another springtime river. The water runs high and fast through March and early April. Then, by the end of April, it is usually so low it is not possible to make the run without a lot of scraping and scratching.

Access

To leave a car at the take-out point, take CT 67 (Exit 15 from I-84) north from Southbury through the village of Roxbury, and then follow it as it bends back south along the river, which will now be on your right. There are several small parking areas beside the river. Any of these can be used as a take-out, although the largest, called Hodge Park, which has a fireplace also, probably provides the best access. CT 67 crosses the river, but do not go as far as the bridge.

Taking out there is not easy. Moreover, a short distance below the bridge there is a dam and beyond that a notorious falls that invites disaster.

On your way to the put-in in Washington Depot, backtrack on CT 67. You can then take the first road left, Sentry Hill Road, for a look at the river a couple of miles upstream. Following the dirt roads beyond that all the way to Washington Depot, however, can be confusing and time consuming. It is better to follow Sentry Hill Road only to the river, check out the water from the bridge, and then return to CT 67. Go left on CT 67 a short distance to CT 199, turn left (north) and drive to the picturesque village of Washington. There, turn left on CT 47 and drive the mile to the bridge over the Shepaug at Washington Depot. Just beyond the bridge, a road runs to the right along the river. Put-in is about a hundred yards down this road, beside an old five-stall garage.

The River

Start/
CT 47
bridge

The early part of this trip is somewhat indicative of what is to come. Good current, shallow water, and a bed of thousands of rocks—the word "Shepaug" means "rocky river"—combine to produce riffles that are a joy to skim over when there is enough water. It will be scratchy here in low water, however. You will leave the village of Washington Depot quickly, although a few houses can be seen along the river on the right for a short distance. A feature of most of this run, impressive stands of hemlock trees, covers the left bank. You will probably see more hemlocks on this trip than on any other in this book.

Just as you swing around the first bend, you will float into a minor set of rapids, perhaps Class II in American Canoe Association ratings. In addition, there are a few other boulder patches to negotiate, but for the most part this early stretch is a quick and easy float. You will pass under the first bridge in a matter of 20 minutes or so, and then come upon a parklike area. A dirt road follows the left shore, and you'll see picnic grills and an occasional outhouse. This area, among southern New England's most beautiful spots with towering hemlocks casting a permanent shadow over moss-covered ledges, belongs to the Steep Rock Association. The campground annually draws hundreds of hikers, horseback riders, and birders. Some canoeists too put in here occasionally. Also in this area is the American Indian Archaeological Institute. The Institute, which is located in the woods on the left side of the river and cannot be seen from the water, exhibits numerous Indian artifacts, a great many of which were found near here. The main entrance to the institute is on CT 199. Throughout the Steep Rock campground, the Shepaug offers stretches of easy riffles punctuated by brief rapids. All can be run without scouting ahead when the water is high enough. The most difficult spot lies in a sharp bend where the

Photographer Millard takes a break beneath a towering hemlock.

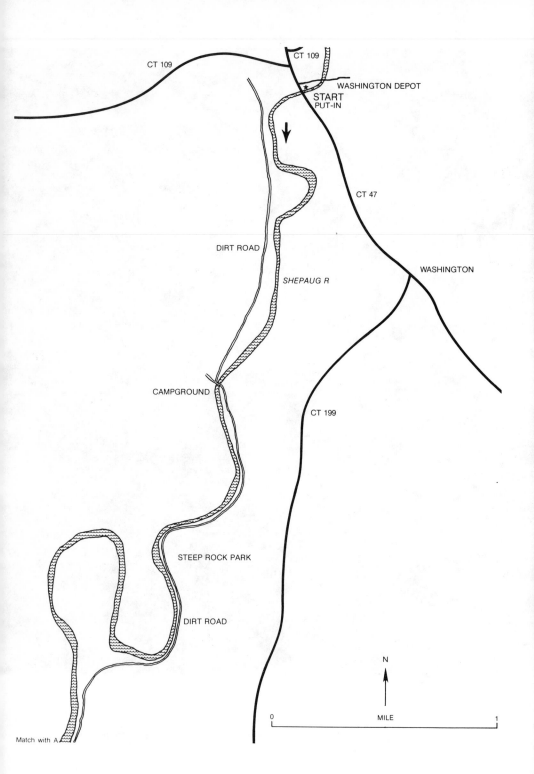

CT 109

CT 109

WASHINGTON DEPOT

START
PUT-IN

CT 47

DIRT ROAD

WASHINGTON

SHEPAUG R

CAMPGROUND

CT 199

STEEP ROCK PARK

DIRT ROAD

N

0   MILE   1

Match with A

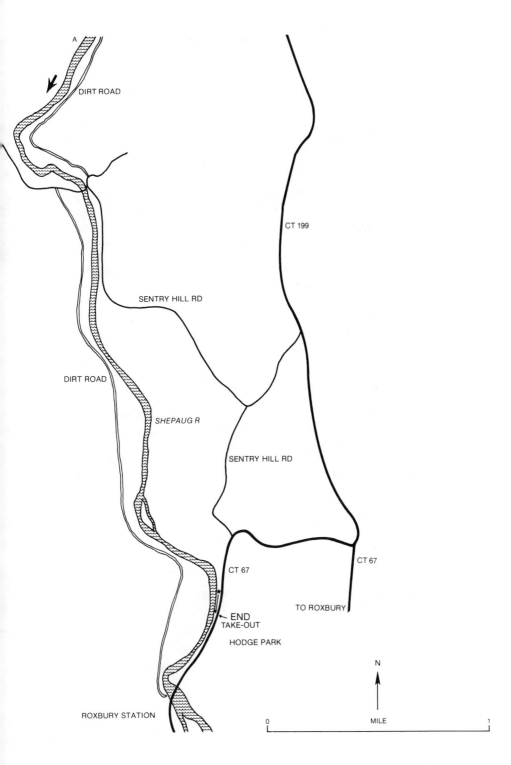

A

DIRT ROAD

CT 199

SENTRY HILL RD

DIRT ROAD

SHEPAUG R

SENTRY HILL RD

CT 67

CT 67

END
TAKE-OUT

TO ROXBURY

HODGE PARK

ROXBURY STATION

N

0   MILE   1

145 *Connecticut*

right bank rises into an awesome moss-draped ledge. A couple of big boulders in the river here can catch unwary canoeists, but you should be able to get through if you stay just right of center. Almost immediately, there is another, longer stretch of rapids. This time the best route is a straight run along the right bank. Then you will be back to alternate patches of riffles and short Class I rapids. None are difficult. Take advantage of one of the quieter segments here to pull ashore for a lunch break among the hemlocks, ferns, and chickadees.

After a series of bends that describe almost a full circle, the highest ledge of the river looms above you on the right. This immense rock is indeed steep—even hemlocks have trouble growing on the wall. The crest of the ledge is nearly 500 feet above the water. It's an awesome sight, but don't spend all of your time looking up, for you are now entering the longest rapids of the trip. This stretch of whitewater extends several hundred yards and is very fast, but not difficult. Just great fun.

As the ridge on the right begins to flatten out, you will notice No Trespassing signs—respect them—and fewer rapids. It is not far now to the next landmark, the final bridge on this run. Just beyond the bridge, on the right, is a large cattle farm. The road on the left is Sentry Hill Road, which you drove earlier when you looked over the river. The valley widens now, and you'll find some oaks, maples, and sycamores along the banks. The ever present hemlocks can still be seen cloaking the hillsides beyond. One huge tree has fallen across the river here, but there is just enough room for a canoe to pass on the extreme right.

Where the river divides around a big island, it is better to go right. The left passage is shorter, but also narrower and shallower, so you are more likely to get hung up there. And on this river, who wants to take short cuts anyway? It is only a short distance to your car from the island. You'll probably wish you were just starting out instead of taking out.

CT 67/
end

Housatonic River—Quickwater

Cornwall Bridge to Kent

Put-in Point	Take-out Point	Approximate Distance	Approximate Trip Time	Condition of Water	Portages
Cornwall Bridge	CT 341 bridge	9½ miles	3-3½ hours	Mostly fast	None

Do this stretch of the Housatonic River in northwestern Connecticut when the water is just right—not too high or too low—and you are likely to be hooked on canoeing for life. This 9½-mile trip has just about everything canoeists seek: enough fast current and rapids for excitement, and periods of calm that allow for relaxed gazing at the shorelines. The shores, too, are made to order with boulders, ledges, and virtually unbroken forest the entire distance of the trip. High wooded hills form the horizons on both sides of the river.

Unlike the Housatonic just a few miles upriver (see Trip 25), however, the section covered here—from Cornwall Bridge west of Cornwall to the town of Kent—undergoes great changes with the seasons and weather conditions. It should never be taken lightly, especially by those not skilled at handling whitewater. In spring and after heavy rainstorms, the river here can be wild and dangerous. In autumn and in extremely dry periods, on the other hand, it can be quite scratchy because of many nearly exposed rocks. The upper Housatonic, even though just a few miles away, remains gentle in all but flooding periods because of the huge dam at Falls Village. The section between Falls Village and Cornwall, which includes a picturesque covered bridge at West Cornwall, is a favorite of whitewater canoeists. That segment is not included here because it requires skills beyond those of the average paddler and also because it cannot be run at all during low-water months.

Access

To make the Cornwall Bridge-to-Kent trip, drive US 7 to the village of Kent, go west on CT 341 a short distance to Elizabeth Street, on the left, before the river. Follow Elizabeth Street to its end at a school. At the rear of a parking lot behind the school you'll find a small landing on the riverbank. This will be your take-out point.

High wooded hills form the horizon on both sides of this stretch of the Housatonic.

Leave a car here and return with your canoe to US 7. Turn north (left) and drive the 8 miles to Cornwall Bridge, where the highway joins CT 4 and turns west over the river. Immediately after crossing the bridge, turn right onto River Road, which swings down under the bridge at the river's shore. You can put in across from a state highway garage if you are careful to park your car out of the way of the state trucks.

The River

Start/
Cornwall
Bridge

The Housatonic at the put-in is typical of the stretch you will be canoeing. It is wide, shallow, and rocky. There is no single channel. Moreover, during times of relatively low water you will have to start rock dodging right away. The current normally is quick but not so swift that it cannot be handled. The river is wide enough to allow you to maneuver around rocks that you cannot float over. In the early going, these patches of riffles alternate with stretches of smooth water. Then, about a mile from the start, the water drops a foot or more over a ledge in the riverbed, and care must be taken in going over. In low water, a liftover may be required. Shortly beyond this ledge, as you round a bend, you will come upon a short rapid between larger rocks. It can be fun to run, but do it on the right.

This is perhaps the most beautiful portion of a truly beautiful river. Tall sycamores, maples, and oaks crowd the shoreline, along with some pines, beeches, and dogwoods. Huge boulders flank the river, particularly on the right, inviting you ashore for lunch or rest breaks. Take a break where you find trails coming down to the water from the right. If you follow the paths back into the woods a few yards, you'll emerge on a well-worn lane. This is a segment of the famed Appalachian Trail that extends from Maine to Georgia. The trail follows the river here for a couple of miles and a stroll along it provides a pleasant interlude. One spot in particular, marked by a brook entering the river from the right, is worth exploring for its extensive stonework in fences, retaining walls, and cellar holes. These remains date from the early days of life on the Housatonic. Today the area belongs to the birds and the squirrels.

Back on the river, you'll resume alternating between rock dodging and easy paddling. Here the smooth stretches become longer, and you'll have more time to take in the scenery. Hawks and ospreys keep watch from the treetops, and during migration times—spring and fall—ducks and geese often congregate in this area. Floating into a flock of sixty Canadian geese on one October trip was the highlight of the day for us. And seeing them clamber off into the sky against a backdrop of wine-red hillside foliage more than made up for all the low-water lining we had to do.

The water is especially shallow around the several islands you'll pass. Choose the side with the fewest riffles, and in most cases under normal water conditions you'll get by. When you begin to see

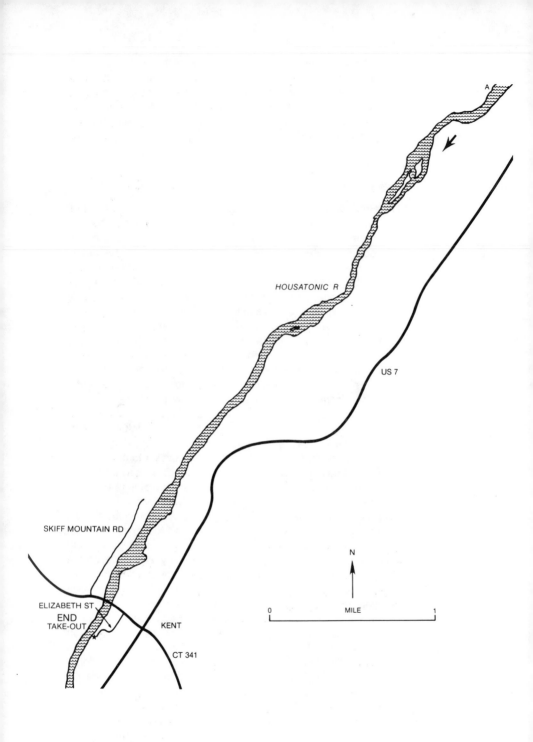

A

HOUSATONIC R

US 7

SKIFF MOUNTAIN RD

ELIZABETH ST
END
TAKE-OUT

KENT

CT 341

N

0   MILE   1

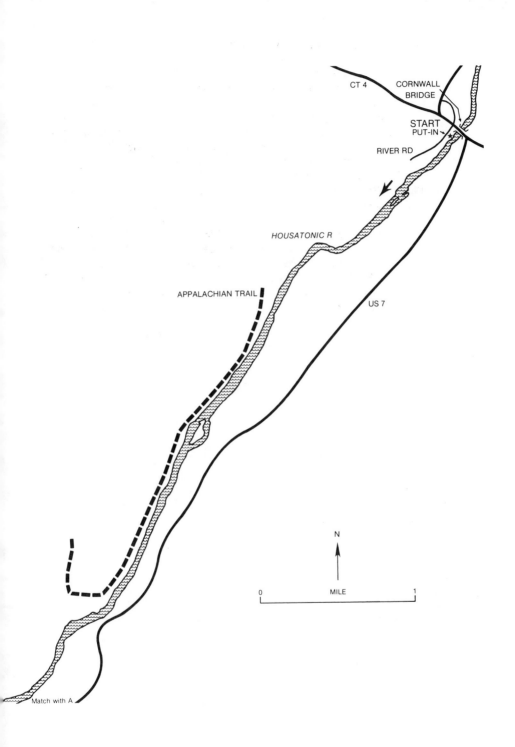

CT 4

CORNWALL
BRIDGE

START
PUT-IN

RIVER RD

HOUSATONIC R

APPALACHIAN TRAIL

US 7

N

0   MILE   1

Match with A

houses on the right shore, the first buildings of any kind since put-in, you are nearing the longest and best (or worst, depending on your point of view) rapids of the trip. Large rocks lie scattered across the river and hundreds of smaller ones rest just below the surface, hidden in the standing waves. Experts may be able to run the full distance without hitting a rock, but most canoeists will bounce off a few here and there. Fortunately, only in high water is this stretch really dangerous. At other times, it's just fun.

CT 341
bridge/
end
The remaining ½ mile is almost anticlimatic. It is all smooth water as you pass the private dock of Kent School on the right, float under the CT 341 bridge, and continue about a hundred yards to your take-out on the left.

As a bonus, the area of this trip is well provided with campgrounds —the Housatonic Meadows State Park (near your start) north of Cornwall, the Macedonia Brook State Park (near take-out) west of Kent, and the Kent Falls State Park, in between on US 7. All do a thriving business during prime canoeing time. After a day on the Housatonic, you'll know why. This is a river you will not want to leave.

Housatonic River—Flatwater

Ashley Falls to Falls Village

Put-in Point	Take-out Point	Approximate Distance	Approximate Trip Time	Condition of Water	Portages
MA 7A bridge	Falls Village Dam	10¼ miles	4½–5 hours	Smooth	Old Canaan Dam

It would be a good idea before making this trip to read the books *This Hill, This Valley* or *Beyond Your Doorstep* by the late naturalist Hal Borland, for this stretch of the Housatonic River runs through the valley he so richly describes. Knowing a bit about the trees, plants, and animals along the river will greatly enhance the enjoyment of this leisurely 10¼-mile trip. You will see otter slides and oriole nests, squirrels in the treetops, swallows over the water, dragonflies hovering above your paddle, ducks hiding in the weeds, mighty maples resplendent in autumn finery, and fragile wildflowers blooming on grassy banks. Borland, whose home you pass midway in the trip, described them all; finding them on your own is like following a treasure map.

This segment of the river, running from just above the Connecticut line in southwestern Massachusetts to Falls Village in Connecticut, is vastly different from the rest of the upper Housatonic. Just a few miles below this stretch (see Trip 24), the Housatonic is a fast and often wild whitewater river. For this entire section, however, except briefly during spring thaws, it is a tranquil, slow-moving waterway that wanders through a farming valley carved into the foothills of the Berkshire Mountains. Even the most inexperienced canoeist will be able to handle this portion of the river. There is one portage, around or over a broken dam, but this is a small price to pay for 4½ or 5 hours of floating pleasure.

Access

To leave a car at your take-out point, drive to Falls Village on CT 126, take Main Street to Water Street, go past a power station, cross the river, and then turn right on Housatonic River Road and continue until you come to a landing beside the power plant dam. This dam creates the smooth water of the trip you are undertaking. Return with your canoe to CT 126, follow it north to US 44, and take that highway into Canaan. Pick up US 7, heading north, here and follow it until reaching 7A, which angles off to the left, just south of the Massachusetts line. Stay on 7A for 2 miles, passing through Ashley Falls. At the river you will find parking space for a few cars just beyond the bridge. The best put-in is over a guard rail on the right.

The River

Start
MA 7A
bridge

After floating under the bridge and a railroad bridge beside it, you'll begin to meander through a series of pastures interrupted by small woodlots. Cattle grazing beneath tall sycamores combine with farmhouses in the distance and wooded hills beyond to form an idyllic setting. You'll find the water almost mirror smooth, but there will be enough current to keep you moving. In less than a mile, you will reach a modern concrete bridge (difficult access) and just beyond that, on the right, the rocky bluffs of Bartholomew's Cobble. This is an intriguing area of knolls and dense forests owned by a conservationist group. Public trails wind through the property; you are likely to see hikers here, particularly in the spring and fall.

The view of the cobble from the river is good at this point, but you will see its ledges and trees even better after completing a big oxbow bend that takes you around a pasture and back toward the cobble. From this far side, especially in autumn, the bluffs are beautiful. A mixture of white birch, pines, maples, and oaks offers a delightful foliage display.

Once you leave the cobble behind, the shorelines flatten out into farming fields behind a thin screen of trees. The river runs wide and smooth here with a few logs and snags, but there is plenty of room to maneuver. Begin looking on your left in this area for otter slides, well-worn paths used by the playful animals in their evening frolicking. You might be lucky enough to see an otter but it is more likely you'll have to settle for the slides and footprints in the mud. A search along the shoreline may turn up other tracks, too—raccoon, fox, muskrat, mink, and skunk—for this valley has an abundance of wildlife.

Shortly after passing a stone abutment in the middle of the river, look for a large weeping willow on the right bank. This is the only large willow in the area. Just beyond the willow, facing the river, stands Borland's house. It is easily seen from the river. Also visible are the sloping fields and hillsides of his books. Do not leave the river here, however, for the banks are private property.

About ½ mile past the Borland farm, you'll come to the old broken Canaan Dam. In high water, you might be able to run over the collapsed right end. The portage path is through the woods on the left. This can be a relatively tough carry, however, so if the water

The view of Bartholomew's Cobble is especially good here near the big oxbow bend.

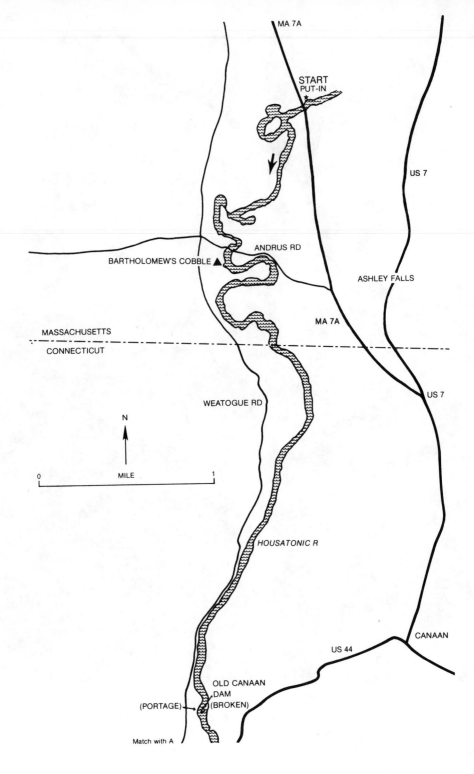

MA 7A

START
PUT-IN

US 7

ANDRUS RD

BARTHOLOMEW'S COBBLE ▲

ASHLEY FALLS

MA 7A

MASSACHUSETTS
CONNECTICUT

US 7

WEATOGUE RD

N

0   MILE   1

HOUSATONIC R

CANAAN

US 44

OLD CANAAN
DAM
(PORTAGE) ← (BROKEN)

Match with A

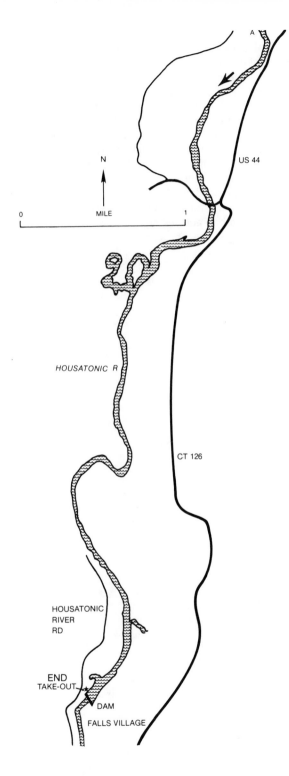

A

N

US 44

0   MILE   1

HOUSATONIC R

CT 126

HOUSATONIC
RIVER
RD

END
TAKE-OUT

DAM

FALLS VILLAGE

157 *Connecticut*

is calm you might be better off just floating up to the center of the dam, lifting over it, carrying across the small island that has formed below the dam, and then putting in again. We have done this without major difficulties.

Your next landmark, less than a mile past the broken dam, is the US 44 bridge (no easy access), about 6½ miles from the start. After this point, the river slows down even more. It may take you 2 hours to paddle the final 4 miles. Unless you are in a hurry you won't mind, because the attractiveness of the shores increases as the valley narrows and the hills draw closer on both sides. Some of the hills **Falls** so high the houses at their bottom, easily seen from the water, are **Village** in shadow by midafternoon. When you begin finding boulders **Dam/** in the riverbed and seeing ledges on shore, you'll be nearing the **end** Falls Village Dam. The take-out is on the right.